MAKING MATHS MEANINGFUL

A Student's Workbook for Mathematics in Class 8

Jamie York

Floris
Books

Contents

To the Student (and Parent)   **3**

Number Bases

Sheet 1a   4
Sheet 1b   5
Sheet 2a   6
Sheet 2b   7
Sheet 3a   8
Sheet 3b   9
Sheet 4a   10
Sheet 4b   12
Sheet 5a   13
Sheet 5b   16
Sheet 6a   17
Sheet 6b   19
Sheet 7a   20
Sheet 7b   21

Pythagorean Theorem

Sheet 1a   23
Sheet 1b   24
Sheet 2a   25
Sheet 2b   26
Sheet 3a   27
Sheet 3b   28
Sheet 4   30
Sheet 5   31

Mensuration

Sheet 1a   32
Sheet 1b   34
Sheet 2a   35
Sheet 2b   36
Sheet 3   37
Sheet 4a   39
Sheet 4b   40
Sheet 5   41
Sheet 6   43

Percentages and Growth

Sheet 1   44
Sheet 1b   46
Sheet 2a   47
Sheet 2b   48

Sheet 3a   50
Sheet 3b   51
Sheet 4   53
Sheet 5   54
Sheet 6   56

Proportions

Sheet 1a   58
Sheet 1b   60
Sheet 2a   61
Sheet 2b   62
Sheet 3a   64
Sheet 3b   65
Sheet 4   67
Sheet 5   68
Sheet 6   70
Sheet 7   71

Algebra

Sheet 1   73
Sheet 2   75
Sheet 3   76
Sheet 4   78
Sheet 5   79
Sheet 6   80

End of Year Review

Sheet 1   82
Sheet 2   83
Sheet 3   85
Sheet 4   86

Multiplication Tables for Number Bases   **88**

Place Value (exponent) Table   **89**

Binary/Hexidecimal Conversion Table   **90**

Table of Squares   **90**

Table of Square Roots   **91**

Growth Rate Table   **92**

Conversion Table   **93**

To the Student (and Parent)

This is the last year before the upper school! Compared to my Class Seven workbook, the practice sheets in this workbook are shorter, but more challenging. And this year, there are group sheets that will stretch you to discover maths more independently. Hard work this year will pay off when you study maths in upper school. Have you thought much about needing to be prepared for upper school maths? Remember that you need three things (1) basic maths skills (learning the material in this workbook is more than adequate), (2) good study skills and (3) enthusiasm for learning maths.

Some tips for using this workbook

- Make sure your work is readable and easy to follow.
- If there isn't enough room on the worksheet, then show your work on a separate sheet of paper, making sure you write down the worksheet number and problem number, so you can easily find it later.
- Answers for division problems may be rounded to three significant digits, unless the problem states you should leave your answer as an exact decimal, in which case you must continue until it repeats or ends. For example, $2579 \div 56$ has an exact answer of $46.053\overline{571428}$. Rounding it to three significant digits means we go to the fourth digit (which is the second place after the decimal point, and is a 5 in this case), and then round up the previous digit for an answer of 46.1.
- Try your best on every problem. Struggling and overcoming frustration are part of the process of doing maths. Even if you don't get a problem correct, you will learn by trying it, and then later seeing a correct solution.
- At the back of this workbook, you will find several tables that will assist you in doing your work.

Getting help

The problems in this workbook are based upon the material found in our book, *A Teacher's Source Book Mathematics: Classes 6–8*. The book has helpful explanations and examples, and is useful for parents (or tutors) who are helping their children with the worksheets found in this workbook.

Number Bases – Sheet 1a

The base-ten and the base-eight number systems

The way in which we count and the way our number system evolved, stems from the fact that people have ten fingers. Therefore, our number system is a base-ten (or decimal) number system, and there are ten digits in this system.

However, it didn't have to be that way. It is perfectly possible to develop a number system different from the one we are used to. That is what this unit will focus on.

We will start with a base-eight, or octal, number system. Imagine that you have a friend, Bob, who only knows this base-eight numbers system. This base-eight system is a place-value, or positional, number system, similar to our base-ten (decimal) system. Also all of its digits are digits that we also use, but it doesn't use some of the digits that we do.

1) Count in the base-eight (or octal) number system until you are ten past the point of needing three digits.

2) What are the digits used in the base-ten (decimal) system?

3) What are the digits used in the base-eight (octal) system?

4) Which digits does the base-ten system have that the base-eight system doesn't?

5) You and Bob are watching over a herd of sheep. You count the sheep in decimal and Bob counts the sheep in octal. Fill out the table, so that for each problem, your number and Bob's number are equivalent – i.e. your number and Bob's number each represent the same number of sheep.

	Bob's number	Your number
a)	15	
b)	22	
c)	35	
d)	53	
e)	77	
f)	100	
g)	127	
h)	302	
i)		19
j)		9
k)		6
l)		56
m)		43
n)		94
o)		344

A Student's Workbook for Mathematics in Class 8

Number Bases – Sheet 1b

The Egyptian number system

This is a non-positional number system.

$|$ = one $\cap$ = ten e = 100

$\mathcal{E}$ = 1000 γ = 10,000 $\mathcal{S}$ = 100,000

Example: 213 can be written in the Egyptian system as $ee\cap|||$ or $\cap|||ee$ or $|||\cap ee$.
The position of the symbols does not matter.

1) Fill in the table.

	Egyptian	decimal	scientific
a)	$\cap\mathcal{E}\mathcal{E}\mathcal{E}$		
b)		2,405	
c)			3.041×10^5
d)		20,050	

2) Convert each number from standard decimal form to expanded notation.
   a) 564

   b) 2,369

   c) 2,400

   d) 56,000,000

   e) 300,400

3) Convert each number from expanded notation to standard decimal form.
   a) $7 \times 10^2 + 9 \times 10^1 + 8 \times 10^0$

   b) $7 \times 10^5 + 3 \times 10^4 + 2 \times 10^3 + 1 \times 10^2 + 4 \times 10^1 + 5 \times 10^0$

   c) $4 \times 10^8 + 6 \times 10^6 + 7 \times 10^4 + 9 \times 10^2 + 8 \times 10^0$

   d) $4 \times 10^7 + 6 \times 10^6$

4) Convert to scientific notation:
   a) 320,000,000

   b) 6078.89

   c) 700,000,000,000

   d) 4 trillion

   e) 20^{10}

5) Convert to standard decimal form.
   a) 5.8×10^6

   b) 2.4038×10^3

   c) 1.83×10^{14}

   d) 4×10^1

   e) 4.39853×10^9

   f) 7.43×10^0

Number Bases – Sheet 2a

1) Convert from octal to decimal.
   (If you get stuck, then try writing it
   in expanded notation first.)

   a) 75_{oct}

   b) 123_{oct}

   c) 270_{oct}

   d) 3046_{oct}

2) Convert from decimal to octal.
   a) 28_{dec}

   b) 70_{dec}

   c) 73_{dec}

   d) 94_{dec}

   e) 164_{dec}

3) Add or subtract. Think only in octal.
   For example, with $6_{oct} + 4_{oct}$, don't
   think that $6 + 4$ is 10 in decimal, and
   convert that into 12 in octal. But rather,
   count in octal four above six: 7, 10, 11,
   12.
   a) 45_{oct}
      $+57_{oct}$

   b) 245_{oct}
      $+716_{oct}$

   c) 73_{oct}
      -27_{oct}

   d) 523_{oct}
      -265_{oct}

4) Fill in the octal multiplication table
   below. Look for patterns and similarity
   with the decimal multiplication table.

	0	1	2	3	4	5	6	7
0								
1								
2								
3								
4								
5								
6								
7								

5) Use the above multiplication table in
   order to multiply. (Check your answer
   by casting out sevens!)
   a) 45_{oct}
      $\times 57_{oct}$

   b) 573_{oct}
      $\times 247_{oct}$

Number Bases – Sheet 2b

1) Fill in the table:

	Egyptian	decimal	scientific
a)			6.02×10^4
b)		350	
c)	⟩⟩⟩⟩𓈙𓋹𓋹|||∩		
d)			3.041×10^3
e)		43,350	

2) Convert to standard decimal form:
a) 5.03×10^5

b) 5.03×10^{-3}

c) 5.03×10^{-9}

d) 5.03×10^0

3) Convert to scientific notation:
a) 65,200

b) 700,000,000

c) 0.000 006 3

d) 8.2

4) Convert to expanded notation.
a) 652

b) 8,327

c) 70,800

5) Convert to standard decimal form:
a) $5 \times 10^2 + 4 \times 10^1 + 3 \times 10^0$

b) $8 \times 10^6 + 3 \times 10^4$

c) $7 \times 10^3 + 2 \times 10^2 + 6 \times 10^0$

6) Write down the four numbers that follow each octal (base-eight) number.
a) 6_{oct}

b) 25_{oct}

c) 46_{oct}

d) 75_{oct}

e) 65_{oct}

f) 146_{oct}

7) Write each octal number in expanded (base-eight) notation.
a) 73_{oct}

b) 163_{oct}

c) 345_{oct}

8) Convert from octal (base-eight) to decimal (base-ten).
a) 37_{oct}

b) 52_{oct}

c) 5_{oct}

d) 107_{oct}

e) 234_{oct}

9) Convert from decimal to octal.
a) 23_{dec}

b) 39_{dec}

c) 67_{dec}

d) 80_{dec}

Number Bases – Sheet 3a

1) Convert from octal to decimal:
a) 246_{oct}

b) 777_{oct}

c) 1000_{oct}

2) Convert from decimal to octal.
a) 87_{dec}

b) 384_{dec}

3) *Octal arithmetic*
a) $\begin{array}{r} 456_{oct} \\ +372_{oct} \\ \hline \end{array}$

b) $\begin{array}{r} 333333_{oct} \\ -55555_{oct} \\ \hline \end{array}$

c) $\begin{array}{r} 46_{oct} \\ \times 57_{oct} \\ \hline \end{array}$

Base-five
4) What are the digits in the base-five system?

5) Count in base-five until you are ten past the point of needing three digits.

6) What are the first four place values of the base-five system? (Write them in decimal.)

7) Convert to decimal:
a) 23_{five}

b) 42_{five}

c) 103_{five}

d) 433_{five}

8) Convert to base-five:
a) 6_{dec}

b) 16_{dec}

c) 58_{dec}

Hexadecimal (base-16)
9) What are the digits in the hexadecimal system?

10) Count in hex up to 30_{hex}.

11) Write down the three numbers that follow each hexadecimal number:
a) 18_{hex}

b) $3E_{hex}$

c) $4A8_{hex}$

d) $29E_{hex}$

e) $6FE_{hex}$

12) What are the first four place values of the hexadecimal system? (Write them in decimal.)

13) Convert to decimal:
a) 23_{hex}

b) $A2_{hex}$

c) $13B_{hex}$

14) Convert to hex:
a) 6_{dec}

b) 28_{dec}

c) 268_{dec}

15) Fill in the table (in normal base ten numbers):

Place value (exponent)

10	9	8	7	6	5	4	3	2	1	0	base
											2
											5
											8
					100,000	10,000	1,000	100	10	1	10
											16

Number Bases – Sheet 3b

1) Convert from octal to decimal (if you get stuck, then try writing it in expanded notation first):

a) 36_{oct}

b) 25_{oct}

c) 67_{oct}

d) 47_{oct}

e) 106_{oct}

f) 236_{oct}

g) 562_{oct}

h) 700_{oct}

2) Write 23456_{oct} in expanded notation and then convert it into decimal.

3) Convert from decimal to octal:

a) 39_{dec}

b) 16_{dec}

c) 8_{dec}

d) 53_{dec}

e) 65_{dec}

f) 128_{dec}

g) 469_{dec}

4) Octal arithmetic! Think only in octal. You may use your octal multiplication table for the multiplication problems.

a) 46_{oct}
$+3_{oct}$

b) 362_{oct}
$+366_{oct}$

c) 42_{oct}
-6_{oct}

d) 452_{oct}
-164_{oct}

e) 46_{oct}
$\times 3_{oct}$

f) 56_{oct}
$\times 37_{oct}$

g) 272_{oct}
$\times 304_{oct}$

h) *Challenge*
$3542_{oct} \div 6_{oct}$

Number Bases – Sheet 4a

1) Write each number in expanded notation and then convert to decimal.

a) 236_{oct}

b) 2431_{five}

c) $3D_{hex}$

d) $AB6_{hex}$

2) Convert 100_{dec} to:

a) Octal

b) Base-five

c) Hexadecimal

Binary (base-two)

3) What are the digits in the binary system?

4) Count in binary until you get to six digits.

5) What are the first ten place values of the binary system? (Write them in decimal.)

6) Convert to decimal:
a) 101_{bin}

b) 1000_{bin}

c) 1110_{bin}

d) 10100_{bin}

7) Convert to binary:
a) 6_{dec}

b) 15_{dec}

c) 16_{dec}

d) 100_{dec}

---

8) Fill in each of the multiplication tables. Look for patterns!
Hexadecimal times table

	0	1	2	3	4	5	6	7	8	9	A	B	C	D	E	F
0																
1																
2																
3																
4																
5																
6																
7																
8																
9																
A																
B																
C																
D																
E																
F																

Binary table

	0	1
0		
1		

Base-five table

	0	1	2	3	4
0					
1					
2					
3					
4					

Number Bases – Sheet 4b

1) Write each number in expanded notation and then convert to decimal:

a) 64_{oct}

b) 364_{oct}

c) 2364_{oct}

d) 324_{five}

e) 33042_{five}

f) $1E_{hex}$

g) 72_{hex}

h) ABC_{hex}

2) Convert to octal:

a) 38_{dec}

b) 91_{dec}

c) 600_{dec}

3) Convert to base-five:

a) 38_{dec}

b) 91_{dec}

c) 600_{dec}

4) Convert to hex:
a) 38_{dec}

b) 91_{dec}

c) 600_{dec}

5) Write down the three numbers that follow each given number:
a) 898_{dec}

b) 898_{hex}

c) 776_{oct}

d) 424_{five}

e) $D9_{hex}$

f) $9FFF_{hex}$

6) Count backwards! Write down the three numbers that precede each given number:
a) 101_{oct}

b) 4701_{oct}

c) 200_{five}

d) $D0_{hex}$

e) 101_{hex}

Number Bases – Sheet 5a

Divisibility rules

For each problem, try to determine what the divisibility rule is. You should look at the times tables. Skip the harder ones and come back to them later.

1) Octal, divisible by 8. (i.e. how can you tell if an octal number is evenly divisible by 8?)

2) Octal, divisible by 4.

3) Octal, divisible by 2.

4) Octal, divisible by 7.

5) Octal, divisible by 64.

6) Base-five, divisible by 5.

7) Base-five, divisible by 4.

8) Base-five, divisible by 2.

9) Base-five, divisible by 25.

10) Binary, divisible by 2.

11) Binary, divisible by 4.

12) Binary, divisible by 8.

13) Hex, divisible by 16.

14) Hex, divisible by 8.

15) Hex, divisible by 4.

16) Hex, divisible by 2.

17) Hex, divisible by 15.

18) Hex, divisible by 3.

19) Hex, divisible by 5.

Arithmetic

20) Consider the problem below. Rewrite it in the following bases:

$$17_{dec}$$
$$\underline{+12_{dec}}$$
$$29_{dec}$$

a) octal.

b) base-five.

c) hexadecimal.

d) binary.

21) 456_{oct}
$\underline{+67_{oct}}$

22) 456_{oct}
$\underline{-67_{oct}}$

23) 456_{oct}
$\underline{\times 67_{oct}}$

24) 413_{five}
$\underline{+34_{five}}$

25) 432_{five}
$\underline{-24_{five}}$

26) 33_{five}
$\underline{\times 42_{five}}$

27) 456_{hex}
$\underline{+67_{hex}}$

28) $E5C_{hex}$
$\underline{-A7_{hex}}$

29) $A6_{hex}$
$\underline{\times 37_{hex}}$

30) 10011_{bin}
$\underline{+10111_{bin}}$

31) Rewrite the above problem in decimal.

32) 11010_{bin}
$\underline{-10011_{bin}}$

33) 10011_{bin}
$\underline{\times 1011_{bin}}$

Maths tricks

34) $65_{dec} \times 11_{dec} =$

35) $65_{oct} \times 11_{oct} =$

36) $65_{hex} \times 11_{hex} =$

37) $31_{five} \times 11_{five} =$

38) $43_{five} \times 11_{five} =$

Number Bases – Sheet 5b

1) Convert to decimal:
a) 507_{oct}

b) 10035_{oct}

c) 20443_{five}

d) AA_{hex}

e) $20B7_{hex}$

f) 101_{bin}

g) 1101_{bin}

h) 110100111_{bin}

2) Convert to octal:
a) 72_{dec}

b) 235_{dec}

3) Convert to base-five:
a) 44_{dec}

b) 313_{dec}

4) Convert to hex:
a) 28_{dec}

b) 163_{dec}

c) $65,570_{dec}$

5) Convert to binary:
a) 7_{dec}

b) 19_{dec}

c) 32_{dec}

d) 67_{dec}

e) 153_{dec}

6) Write down the three numbers that follow each given number.

a) 775_{oct}

b) 3243_{five}

c) 998_{hex}

d) $4FFD_{hex}$

e) 101_{bin}

f) 10110_{bin}

7) Count backwards. Write down the three numbers that precede each given number.

a) 7401_{oct}

b) 1000_{five}

c) $9A1_{hex}$

d) $B400_{hex}$

e) 101_{bin}

f) 11101_{bin}

8) *Challenge*

The place value table (see earlier Sheet 3a, p. 8) is completely written in decimal. Rewrite it so that each row is written in its own base.

Place value (exponent)

10	9	8	7	6	5	4	3	2	1	0	base
											2
											5
											8
					100,000	10,000	1,000	100	10	1	10
											16

Number Bases – Sheet 6a

1) Convert to decimal (there is a trick that makes them all easy):

a) 77_{oct}

b) 777_{oct}

c) 7777_{oct}

d) 77777_{oct}

e) 444_{five}

f) 44444_{five}

g) FF_{hex}

h) FFF_{hex}

i) $FFFF_{hex}$

k) 1111_{bin}

l) 11111_{bin}

m) 111111111_{bin}

2) Calculate in the base indicated:
a) $(5_{oct})^3$

b) $\sqrt{10_{hex}}$

c) $\sqrt{100_{hex}}$

d) $\sqrt{1000_{hex}}$

3) Assume that you need to invent a type of Morse code where each character (e.g. a letter) is represented by a certain number of long or short beeps.
Example: How many different characters can be represented if there are 2 beeps per character?
Answer: 4. (The 4 different characters are long-long, long-short, short-long, short-short.)

How many different characters can be represented if there are:
a) 3 beeps per character?

b) 4 beeps per character?

c) 5 beeps per character?

d) 6 beeps per character?

e) 7 beeps per character?

f) 8 beeps per character?

4) What is the minimum number of beeps per character that would be needed in order to represent all the letters and digits?

5) With computers, we speak of bits instead of 'beeps'. A bit can be thought of as a switch. Instead of hearing a long or short beep, a computer 'sees' whether each bit is 'on' or 'off'. A byte is simply a collection of eight bits, which is used to represent one character. A kilobyte is 2^{10} ($\approx 1,000$) bytes. A megabyte is 2^{20} ($\approx 1,000,000$) bytes. A gigabyte is 2^{30} ($\approx 1,000,000,000$) bytes.
a) How many different characters can be represented by one byte?

b) How many bytes of computer memory are needed to store one page of plain text? (Given 6 characters per word, 15 words per line and 50 lines per page.)

c) Your answer above is equal to how many kilobytes?

d) One gigabyte is enough to store about how many pages of plain text?

Number Bases – Sheet 6b

1) Convert to decimal:
a) 4032_{oct}

b) 4032_{hex}

c) 4032_{five}

d) 11011001_{bin}

2) Convert 229_{dec} into:
a) Octal

b) Hexadecimal

c) Base-five

d) Binary

3) $\begin{aligned} 5637_{oct} \\ +4136_{oct} \end{aligned}$

4) $\begin{aligned} 5072_{oct} \\ -674_{oct} \end{aligned}$

5) $\begin{aligned} 526_{oct} \\ \times 45_{oct} \end{aligned}$

6) $\begin{aligned} 33333_{five} \\ +44444_{five} \end{aligned}$

7) $\begin{aligned} 3333_{five} \\ -444_{five} \end{aligned}$

8) $\begin{aligned} 33_{five} \\ \times 44_{five} \end{aligned}$

9) $\begin{aligned} AAAA_{hex} \\ +CCCC_{hex} \end{aligned}$

10) $\begin{aligned} EB9_{hex} \\ -2A_{hex} \end{aligned}$

11) $\begin{aligned} CD_{hex} \\ \times 78_{hex} \end{aligned}$

12) $\begin{aligned} 10101_{bin} \\ +10111_{bin} \end{aligned}$

13) $\begin{aligned} 10110_{bin} \\ -1011_{bin} \end{aligned}$

14) $\begin{aligned} 11001_{bin} \\ \times 101_{bin} \end{aligned}$

15) *Challenge*
$13632_{oct} \div 23_{oct}$

16) *Challenge*
$DD25_{hex} \div A7_{hex}$

Number Bases – Sheet 7a

1) Translate each string of ASCII code into characters using your ASCII table (at the back of this book, p. 89).
   Example: 01001011

   The first four bits are 0100, which is 4 in hex, and the next four bits are 1011, which is B in hex. So we look up 4B from the ASCII table and get K.

   a) 01011101

   b) 01110000

   c) 00111000

   d) 00100000

   e) 01001001, 01110011, 00100000, 01110100, 01101000, 01101001, 01110011, 00100000, 01100110, 01110101, 01101110, 00111111.

2) Write the binary ASCII code for 'Nancy'.

3) If we look at the 2 times table (in decimal) we have 2, 4, 6, 8, 10, 12, 14, 16, etc. We can see that there is a pattern with the last digit and represent this geometrically as:

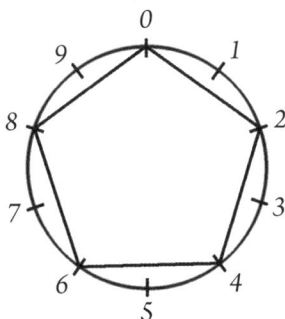

State what each table, below, looks like geometrically:

a) The 4× table in decimal

b) The 6× table in decimal

c) The 8× table in decimal

d) The 2× table in octal

e) The 4× table in octal

f) The 6× table in octal

g) The 2× table in hex

h) The 4× table in hex

i) The 6× table in hex

j) The 8× table in hex

k) The A× table in hex

l) The C× table in hex

m) The E× table in hex

4) *Math tricks.* Use a times table, when helpful.

a) $67.32_{dec} \times 1000_{dec}$

b) $6C.A7_{hex} \times 1000_{hex}$

c) $120{,}000_{dec} \div 30_{dec}$

d) $C0000_{hex} \div 30_{hex}$

e) $103_{dec} \times 105_{dec}$

f) $103_{oct} \times 105_{oct}$

g) $56_{dec} \times 11_{dec}$

h) $56_{oct} \times 11_{oct}$

i) $56_{hex} \times 11_{hex}$

j) $5004_{dec} - 4997_{dec}$

k) $5004_{hex} - 4FF7_{hex}$

l) $4_{dec} \times 99,999_{dec}$

m) $4_{hex} \times FFFFF_{hex}$

n) $51_{dec} \times 49_{dec}$

o) $51_{oct} \times 47_{oct}$

p) $(61_{dec})^2$

q) $(61_{hex})^2$

r) $43_{dec} \times 47_{dec}$

s) $43_{hex} \times 4D_{hex}$

Number Bases – Sheet 7b

1) Translate each string of ASCII code into characters using your ASCII table (at the back of this book).

a) 01101101

b) 01001101

c) 00111101

2) Write the binary ASCII code for 'Mr. Sims'.

3) Translate the following ASCII code and then solve the resulting riddle.
01010111, 01101000, 01100001,
01110100, 00100000, 01100010,
01100001, 01110011, 01100101,
00100000, 01101001, 01110011,
00100000, 01110100, 01101000,
01101001, 01110011, 00111010,
00100000, 00110011, 00110100,
00101011, 00110100, 00110100,
00111101, 00110001, 00110000,
00110000, 00111111

4) 100 gigabytes of computer memory is about how many bytes?

5) Write each decimal number in scientific notation:
a) 67,300,000,000

b) 70,000

c) 0.000 008 32

6) Write each number in standard decimal form:
a) 6.03×10^4

b) 6.03×10^{-3}

c) 6.03×10^0

7) Write down the three numbers that follow each given number:
a) 75_{oct}

b) $9D_{hex}$

c) 444_{five}

d) 11101_{bin}

8) Convert 145_{dec} to:
a) Octal

b) Base-five

c) Hexadecimal

d) Binary

9) Convert to decimal:
a) 10723_{oct}

b) $1A05E_{hex}$

c) 24302_{five}

d) 100101011_{bin}

10) $\begin{array}{r} 4641_{oct} \\ -\,2675_{oct} \end{array}$

11) $\begin{array}{r} 37_{oct} \\ \times\,62_{oct} \end{array}$

12) $\begin{array}{r} 4234_{five} \\ +\,2142_{five} \end{array}$

13) $\begin{array}{r} 32_{five} \\ \times\,43_{five} \end{array}$

14) $\begin{array}{r} 569_{hex} \\ -\,28A_{hex} \end{array}$

15) $\begin{array}{r} 2D6_{hex} \\ \times\ \ 53_{hex} \end{array}$

16) $\begin{array}{r} 110110_{bin} \\ +\,101111_{bin} \end{array}$

17) $\begin{array}{r} 10110_{bin} \\ \times\ \ \ \,101_{bin} \end{array}$

Pythagorean Theorem – Sheet 1a

Note: Throughout this whole unit, when calculating the decimal approximation for a square root, answers should be rounded to three significant digits, unless stated otherwise.

1) Use the square root algorithm to calculate each of the following.

a) $\sqrt{613,089}$

b) $\sqrt{1004.89}$

c) $\sqrt{71}$

2) For each problem below, use a compass and a straightedge to construct a triangle (on a separate piece of paper) that has sides equal to the three given line segments. Then, use a protractor to find the measure of the resulting triangle's three angles.

a) _____

b) _____

c) _____

3) Notice that for the above problem, each of the three triangles has the same length for their shortest side and the same length for their middle-sized side.

a) Describe how the angles change as the longest side gets longer (until no triangle can be formed)?

b) The Pythagorean Theorem says something about one of the three triangles. Which triangle is it, and what does it say?

4) With each triangle, calculate the length of the missing side, *X*.

a)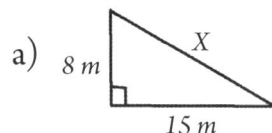
8 m, 15 m, X

b)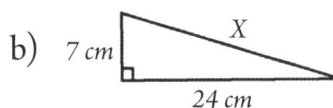
7 cm, 24 cm, X

c)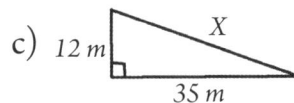
12 m, 35 m, X

Pythagorean Theorem – Sheet 1b

1) Use the square root algorithm to calculate each of the following (each answer is a whole number):

   a) $\sqrt{5776}$

   b) $\sqrt{222{,}784}$

   c) $\sqrt{6{,}568{,}969}$

2) Calculate the length of x:

   a)

   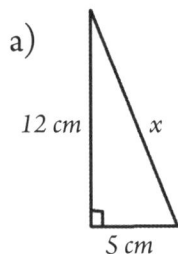

   12 cm, 5 cm, x

   b)

   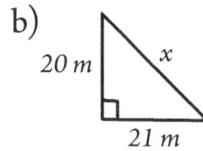

   20 m, 21 m, x

   c)

   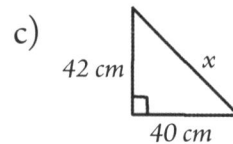

   42 cm, 40 cm, x

3) State what the Pythagorean Theorem says and what it means.

4) *Challenge*
   Calculate $\sqrt{21}$, rounding your answer to six significant digits.

Pythagorean Theorem – Sheet 2a

1) Use the square root algorithm to calculate each of the following.

a) $\sqrt{3}$

b) $\sqrt{5}$

c) $\sqrt{6}$

d) $\sqrt{2}$ (round to six significant digits.)

2) Fill in the blanks with greater than, or less than or equal to.

a) In any *right* triangle, the square of the hypotenuse is ____ the sum of the squares of the other two sides.

b) In any *obtuse* triangle, the square of the hypotenuse is ____ the sum of the squares of the other two sides.

c) In any *acute* triangle, the square of the hypotenuse is ____ the sum of the squares of the other two sides.

3) Below, you are given the length of the three sides of a triangle. State whether the triangle is right, obtuse or acute. (You may use the *Table of squares,* p. 90.)

a) $a = 15$; $b = 20$; $c = 20$

b) $a = 15$; $b = 20$; $c = 25$

c) $a = 15$; $b = 20$; $c = 30$

d) $a = 28$; $b = 96$; $c = 100$

e) $a = 7$; $b = 8$; $c = 11$

f) $a = 5$; $b = 6$; $c = 7$

g) $a = 3$; $b = 4$; $c = 5$

h) $a = 2$; $b = 3$; $c = 4$

4) A Pythagorean triple is three whole numbers that can be the lengths of the three sides of a right triangle. All of the primitive (i.e. reduced) Pythagorean triples that are less than 100 are listed at the back of the book next to the *Table of squares* (p. 90).
Use Pythagorean triples to determine the length of x.

a)

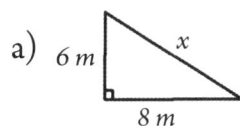

b)

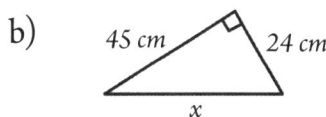

c)

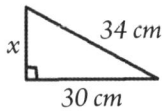
34 cm, x, 30 cm

b)

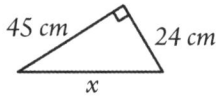
3 m, x, 5 m

5) Use the formula $c^2 = a^2 + b^2$ in order to find x.

c)

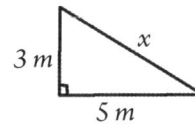
12.4 m, 5.1 m, x

a)

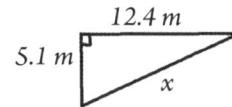
45 cm, 24 cm, x

Pythagorean Theorem – Sheet 2b

1) Use the square root algorithm to calculate each of the following:

a) $\sqrt{7}$

b) $\sqrt{8}$

c) $\sqrt{10}$

2) What is special about a Pythagorean triple?

3) What does the formula $c^2 = a^2 + b^2$ mean and how is it used?

4) Find x (hint: the lengths of the sides are a Pythagorean triple):

a)

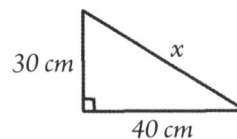
30 cm, x, 40 cm

b)

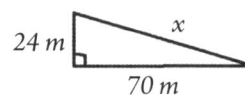
24 m, x, 70 m

c)

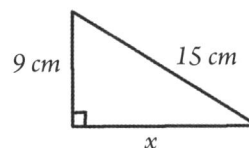
9 cm, 15 cm, x

5) Use $c^2 = a^2 + b^2$ in order to find x:

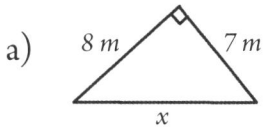

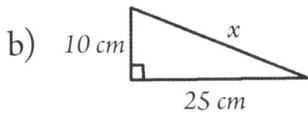

a)

8 m   7 m

x

b)

10 cm   x

25 cm

6) Do each problem first by using Pythagorean triples, and then check your answer by redoing the problem using the formula $c^2 = a^2 + b^2$.

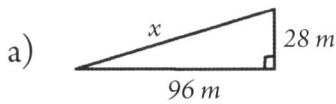

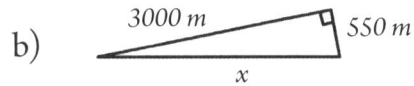

a)

x   28 m

96 m

b)

3000 m   550 m

x

7) *Challenge*
Find w, x, y, z:

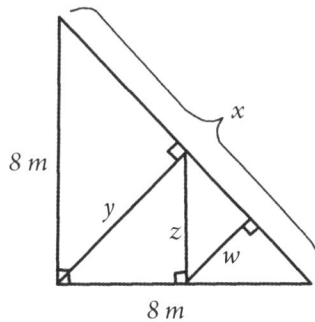

8 m

y

z

w

x

8 m

Pythagorean Theorem – Sheet 3a

Note: The table of squares and square roots may be used on all sheets from here on.

1) $c^2 = a^2 + b^2$ is used to calculate the length of a right triangle's hypotenuse (c) when both of the legs (a and b) are known.

What is the formula that can be used to calculate the length of one leg, when the other leg and the hypotenuse are known?

2) Make sure that the above formula is correct, and then use it to find x.

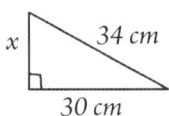

x   34 cm

30 cm

3) Calculate the length of the diagonal of a rectangle that measures 1.5 m by 2 m.

4) Find x, either by using the formula $c^2 = a^2 + b^2$, or the one that you found in 1).

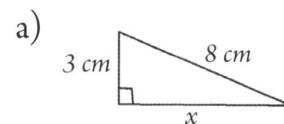

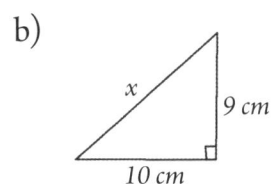

a)

3 cm   8 cm

x

b)

x   9 cm

10 cm

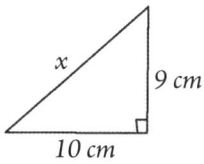

9 cm
x
10 cm

c)

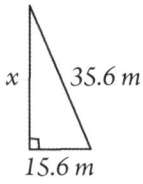

x   35.6 m
15.6 m

6)   *Challenge*
     Find x.

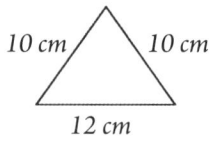

1 m
x
1 m
1 m
1 m
1 m

d)   Calculate the height of this triangle:

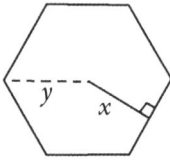

10 cm   10 cm
12 cm

5)   Calculate the long radius (y) and the short radius (x) of a regular hexagon that has 4 cm long sides.

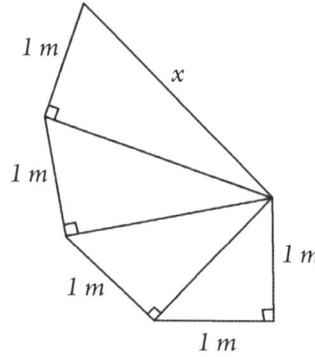

y   x

Pythagorean Theorem – Sheet 3b

1)   Find x, either by using the hypotenuse formula $c^2 = a^2 + b^2$, or the leg formula $a^2 = c^2 - b^2$ or Pythagorean triples.

a)

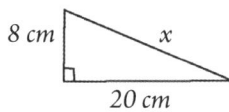

8 cm   x
20 cm

b)

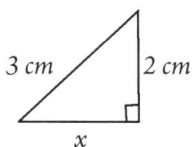

3 cm   2 cm
x

c)

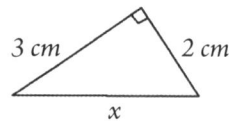

3 cm   2 cm
x

d)

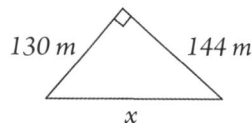

130 m   144 m
x

2) Calculate the exact value, using the square root algorithm, if necessary:
a) Calculate the length of the diagonal of a rectangle that measures 2 m by 1 m.

b) Calculate the height of an equilateral triangle with 8 metre long edges.

c) Calculate the height of this triangle.

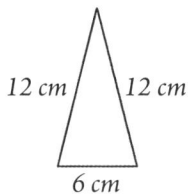

12 cm   12 cm

6 cm

3) *Challenge*
The body diagonal of a cube is the line that goes from one corner of the cube, through its centre and then to the opposite corner. What is the length of the body diagonal of a cube with one metre long edges?

4) Below, you are given the length of the three sides of a triangle. State whether the triangle is right, obtuse or acute.
a) $a = 12$; $b = 20$; $c = 25$

b) $a = 7$; $b = 2.4$; $c = 7$

c) $a = 7$; $b = 2.4$; $c = 7.4$

d) $a = 7$; $b = 2.4$; $c = 8$

e) $a = 36$; $b = 23$; $c = 40$

5) On previous sheets you have calculated the values of the square roots of 2 up through 10. You should now memorise them, since they occur frequently.
They are:
$\sqrt{2} \approx 1.414$ $\qquad$ $\sqrt{6} \approx 2.45$
$\sqrt{3} \approx 1.73$ $\qquad$ $\sqrt{7} \approx 2.65$
$\sqrt{5} \approx 2.24$ $\qquad$ $\sqrt{10} \approx 3.16$
$\sqrt{8} \approx 2.83\ (= 2\sqrt{2})$

Pythagorean Theorem – Sheet 4

1) Find x, either by using the hypotenuse formula $c^2 = a^2 + b^2$, or the leg formula $a^2 = c^2 - b^2$.

a)

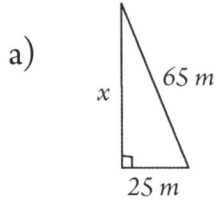

x 65 m

25 m

b)

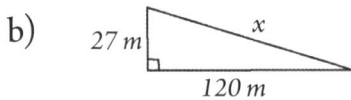

27 m x

120 m

c)

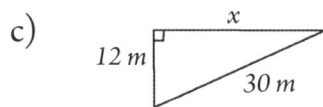

x

12 m

30 m

d) Calculate the height:

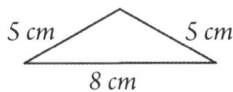

5 cm   5 cm

8 cm

2) Calculate $\sqrt{19}$ rounded to five significant digits.

3) Calculate the length of the diagonal of a square that has sides with a length of:

a) 4 cm

b) 5½ m.

4) Find x.

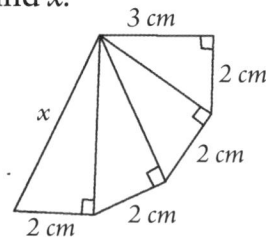

3 cm

2 cm

x

2 cm

2 cm

2 cm

5) *Challenge*
Find a shortcut or a formula to do the above problem more quickly.

6) A rhombus has edges of length $\sqrt{3}$ metres and its short diagonal is 2 m long. How long is its long diagonal?

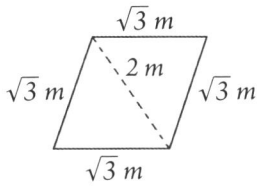

$\sqrt{3}\ m$

$2\ m$

$\sqrt{3}\ m$ $\sqrt{3}\ m$

$\sqrt{3}\ m$

7) *Challenge*
A pyramid has a square base, and all of its edges are 20 m long. Calculate the height of the pyramid.

Pythagorean Theorem – Sheet 5

1) Circle those that can be done using Pythagorean triples, and then solve them. Do the others by using either the leg formula or the hypotenuse formula.

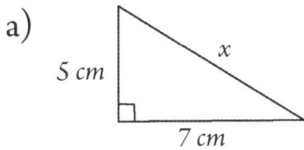

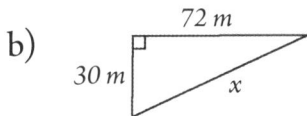

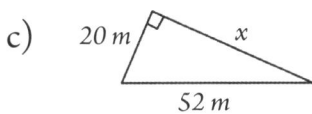

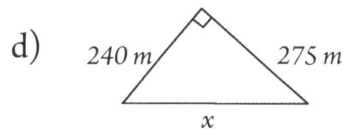

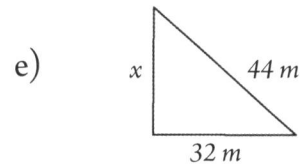

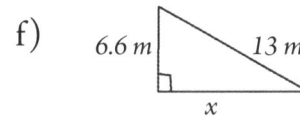

a)

5 cm

x

7 cm

b)

72 m

30 m

x

c)

20 m   x

52 m

d)

240 m   275 m

x

e)

x   44 m

32 m

f)

6.6 m   13 m

x

g) Calculate the height.

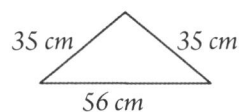

35 cm   35 cm

56 cm

2) Below, you are given the length of the three sides of a triangle. State whether the triangle is right, obtuse or acute.

a) $a = 6$; $b = 12$; $c = 14$

b) $a = 25$; $b = 20$; $c = 30$

c) $a = 3.9$; $b = 8$; $c = 8.9$

3) Use the square root algorithm to calculate $\sqrt{24,700,900}$.

4) Find x.

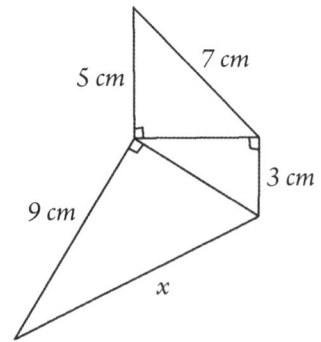

5 cm, 7 cm, 3 cm, 9 cm, x

5) *Challenge*
   Calculate the perimeter of a square that has a 6 metre long diagonal.

Mensuration – Sheet 1a

Note: In this entire unit, you are allowed to use the table of square roots found at the back of this book (p. 91). However, you will need to use the square root algorithm to calculate the square roots of numbers greater than 100.

1) Find the variables:
a) (Two of the lines are parallel.)

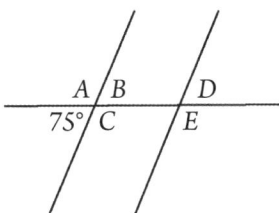

A, B, C, D, E, 75°

b)

51°, X

c)

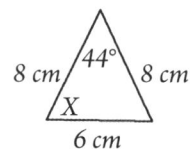

8 cm, 44°, 8 cm, X, 6 cm

2) In this parallelogram, what is the sum of the measures of the four angles?

3) Calculate the area:

a)

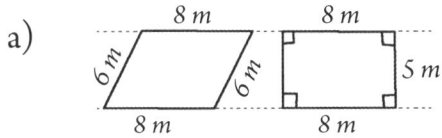

b)

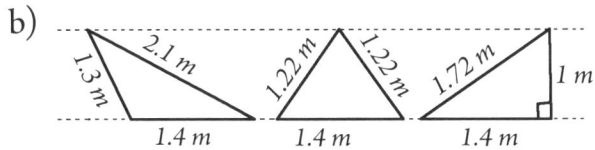

4) The four ratios of a circle are:
$$C:D \approx 22:7$$
$$D:C \approx 7:22$$
$$C:D \approx 3.14:1$$
$$D:C \approx 0.318:1$$
Answer each question using one of the above ratios.

a) What is the circumference of a circle that has a diameter of 35 m?

b) What is the circumference of a circle that has a diameter of 3 m?

c) What is the diameter of a circle that has a circumference of 44 m?

d) What is the diameter of a circle that has a circumference of 20 m?

5) Calculate the area:

a)

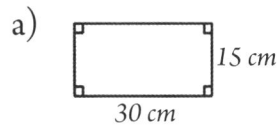

b)

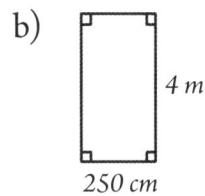

c)

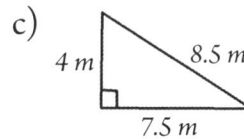

d)

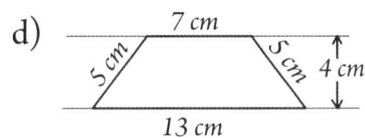

e)

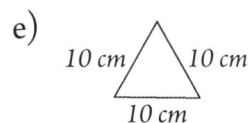

Mensuration – Sheet 1b

The area of a circle

1) With a compass, construct 3 circles that have a radius of about 5 cm. Shade in the inside edge of each circle's circumference with a coloured pencil. Cut the first circle into 4 equal-sized pie pieces, the second one into 8 pieces and the third one into 16 pieces. In each case, put the pieces side by side alternating top and bottom. The first one should look like this:

a) What happens as the circle is cut into more and more pieces?

b) What shape results from having the circle cut into infinitely many pie pieces?

c) What is the area of this final shape, and also, therefore, the area of the circle?

d) What is the formula for the area, A, of a circle, given just the radius, r?

Calculating volume

2) A room has a floor that measures 8 metres by 6 metres, and has a height of 3 metres.
a) What is the area of the floor?

b) What is the volume of water needed to fill the room to a depth of 1 metre?

c) What is the volume of water needed to fill the room to a depth of 2 metres?

d) What is the volume of water needed to fill the room to the ceiling?

3) Given this triangular prism:
a) What is the area of the triangular floor?

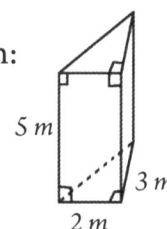

b) What is the volume of the whole prism?

4) By looking at the volumes calculated in the previous two problems, give a formula that can be used to calculate the volume, V, of a solid that has the same top and bottom.

5) Use the above formula to calculate the volume of this box.

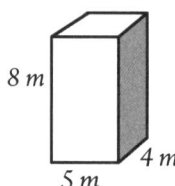

6) Use the formula from 1) d) to calculate the area of this circle.

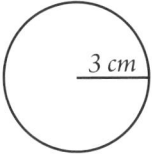
3 cm

7) A box measures 2 m × 2 m × 3 m. It fits perfectly in the corner of a room such that its top is on the ceiling of the room. If the square top of the box slides along the ceiling, thereby stretching the sides of the box (which are flexible), what happens to the volume of the box?

Mensuration – Sheet 2a

1) Calculate the area of each circle. Give your answers both in decimal form to 3 significant figures (using π ≈ 3.14) and in fraction form (using π ≈ $^{22}/_7$).

a)

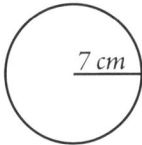
7 cm

b)

8 cm

2) Calculate the area:

a)

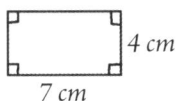
4 cm
7 cm

b)

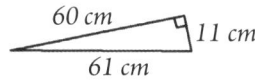
60 cm
11 cm
61 cm

c)

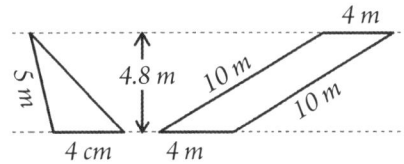
5 m
4.8 m
10 m
4 m
4 cm
4 m
10 m
4 m

d)

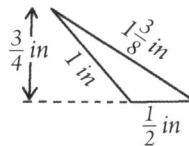
$\frac{3}{4}$ in
1 in
$1\frac{3}{8}$ in
$\frac{1}{2}$ in

e)

12 m
15 m

f)

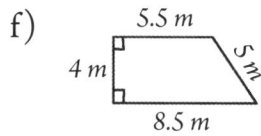
5.5 m
4 m
8.5 m
5 m

g)

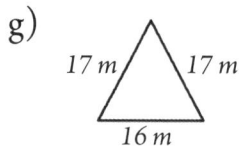
17 m / 17 m
16 m

h)

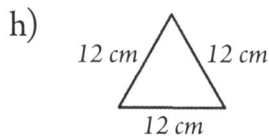
12 cm / 12 cm
12 cm

3) Calculate the volume:

a)

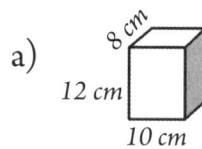
8 cm
12 cm
10 cm

b)

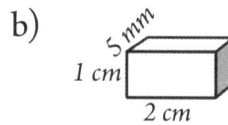
5 mm
1 cm
2 cm

c)

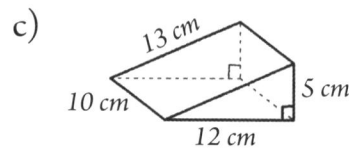
13 cm
10 cm
5 cm
12 cm

Mensuration – Sheet 2b

Volume of a pyramid or cone

We have seen the formula $V = A_{base} \times h$, which is used for calculating the volume of a box, a prism (e.g. triangular) or a cylinder.

Around 430 BC Democritus, a Greek, discovered that the volume of a pyramid is exactly ⅓ the volume of the box that it fits into (i.e. they have the same base and height). Similarly, the volume of a cone is ⅓ the volume of the cylinder that it fits into.

This gives us the formula:

$V = \tfrac{1}{3} A_{base} \times h$

1) Calculate the volume of each solid:
a) A pyramid has a total height of 75 metres, and its square base measures 100 metres on each side.

b) A cone.

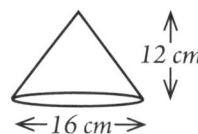
12 cm
←16 cm→

2) Surface area is the sum of all of the areas of the faces that make up a solid. Calculate the volumes and surface area:

a)

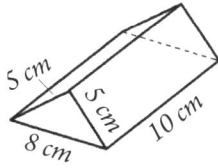

b)

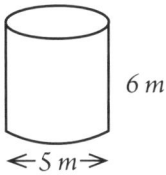

3) a) How many square centimetres are in a square metre?

b) How many cubic centimetres are in a cubic metre?

4) Jon has a cylinder, a sphere and a cone that all have the same diameter and height. He calculates that the volume of each solid is 165 cm³, 110 cm³ and 55 cm³, respectively.

a) What is the ratio of the volume of the cylinder to the sphere to the cone? (This ratio is known as Archimedes' ratio. He discovered it around 250 BC.)

b) What is the volume of a sphere that has a diameter of 18 cm?

Mensuration – Sheet 3

1) The formula $V = A_{\text{base}} \times h$ is used for what?

2) The formula $V = \frac{1}{3}A_{\text{base}} \times h$ is used for what?

3) a) How many square feet are in a square yard?

b) How many cubic feet are in a cubic yard?

c) How many square centimetres are in a square metre?

d) How many cubic centimetres are in a cubic metre?

4) Calculate the area:

a)

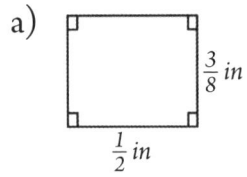
$\frac{3}{8}$ in
$\frac{1}{2}$ in

b)

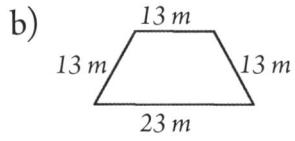
13 m
13 m   13 m
23 m

c)

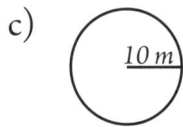
10 m

d)

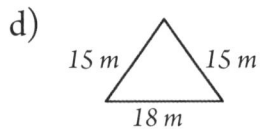
15 m   15 m
18 m

e)

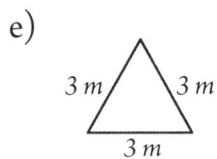
3 m   3 m
3 m

5) Calculate the volume:

a)

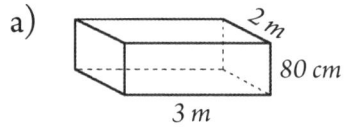
2 m
80 cm
3 m

b)

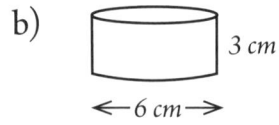
3 cm
←6 cm→

c)

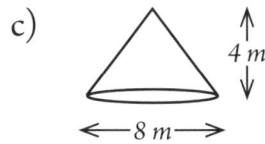
4 m
←8 m→

d)

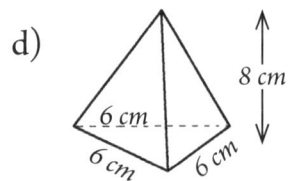
8 cm
6 cm
6 cm   6 cm

e) *Challenge*

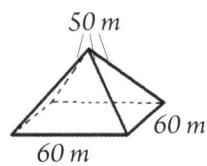
50 m
60 m
60 m

Mensuration – Sheet 4a

1) Calculate the area:

a)

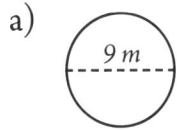
9 m

b)

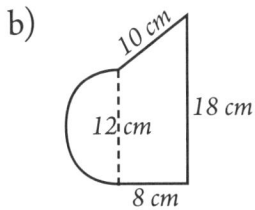
10 cm
12 cm
18 cm
8 cm

c)

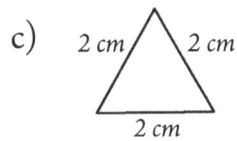
2 cm   2 cm
2 cm

2) Given this portion of a circle:

75°
10 m

a) Calculate the arc length.

b) Calculate the area of the segment of the circle.

3) Calculate the volume:

a)

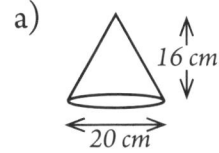
16 cm
20 cm

b)

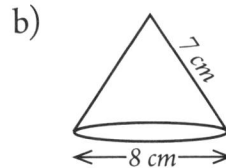
7 cm
8 cm

c)

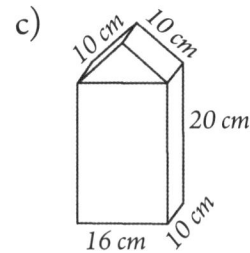
10 cm   10 cm
20 cm
16 cm   10 cm

d) *Challenge*

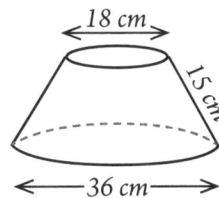
18 cm
15 cm
36 cm

4) Calculate the volume and surface area:

a)

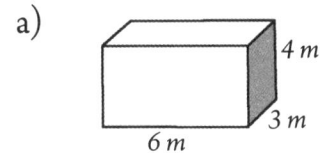
4 m
3 m
6 m

b)

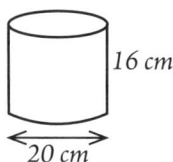
16 cm
20 cm

c)

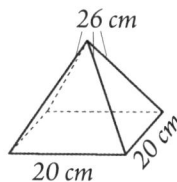
26 cm
20 cm
20 cm

Mensuration – Sheet 4b

Volume and surface area of a sphere

The formula for the volume of a sphere (which can be derived from Archimedes' ratio) is:

$$V = \frac{4}{3}\pi r^3$$

The formula for the surface area of a sphere is:

$$S = 4\pi r^2$$

1) a) Calculate the volume of a ball that has a 12 cm diameter.

   b) Calculate the surface area of a ball that has a 12 cm diameter.

Heron's formula

This formula allows us to calculate the area of a triangle without knowing what the height is. It is:

$$A = \sqrt{s(s-a)(s-b)(s-c)}$$

where a, b, c are the sides of the triangle, and s is the semi-perimeter (i.e. half the length of the perimeter).

Example: Calculate the area of a triangle that has sides of length 7 m, 8 m and 9 m.

The perimeter is 24 m, so the semi-perimeter is 12 m. Putting all the numbers into the formula, we get:

$$\text{Area} = \sqrt{12(12-7)(12-8)(12-9)}$$

which is $\sqrt{12 \times 5 \times 4 \times 3}$, and then $\sqrt{720}$. Using the square root algorithm, we get an area of 26.83 m².

2) Calculate the area:

a)

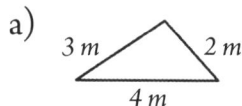
3 m
2 m
4 m

b)

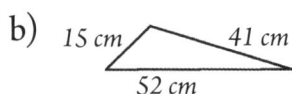
15 cm
41 cm
52 cm

Area efficiency

3) You are given 120 m of fence. How much area is enclosed by the fence if the fence forms the shape of:

a) a square?

b) an equilateral triangle?

c) a regular hexagon?

d) a circle?

e) Which shape encloses area the most efficiently?

Mensuration – Sheet 5

1) Given this portion of a circle:

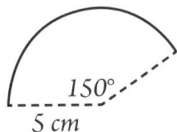
150°
5 cm

a) Calculate the arc length.

b) Calculate the area of the segment of the circle.

2) Calculate the area:

a)

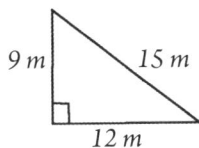
9 m   15 m
12 m

b)

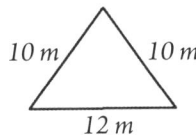
10 m   10 m
12 m

3) Use Heron's formula to calculate the area:

a)

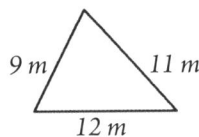
9 m   11 m
12 m

b)

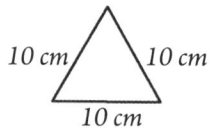

10 cm   10 cm
  10 cm

4) Calculate the volume and surface area of each solid:

a) A box.

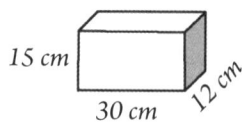

15 cm   12 cm
   30 cm

b) A cylinder.

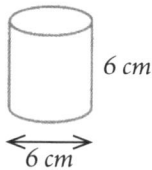

6 cm
6 cm

c) The Earth, which has a diameter of about 12,800 km.

5) Calculate the volume of each solid:

a) A cone.

13 cm
13.2 cm

`b) A 'pointed' cylinder.

10 cm
20 cm
16 cm

c) A pyramid.

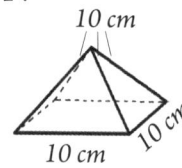

10 cm
10 cm   10 cm

d) *Challenge*
A tetrahedron with all edges 10 cm long.

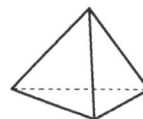

Mensuration – Sheet 6

1) Given a cube with edges 50 cm long:
a) Calculate the volume. Give your answer both in m^3 and cm^3.

b) Calculate the surface area. Give your answer both in m^2 and cm^2.

2) Given this portion of a circle:
a) Calculate the arc length.

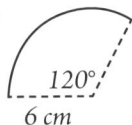
120°
6 cm

b) Calculate the area of the segment of the circle.

3) Calculate the volume and surface area:
a)

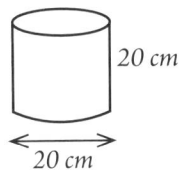
20 cm
20 cm

b) A sphere with a diameter of 20 cm.

c)

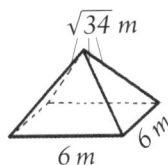
$\sqrt{34}$ m
6 m
6 m

4) Calculate the volume:
a)

29 m
42 m

b)

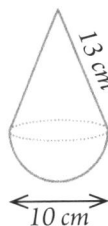
13 cm
10 cm

5) A room measuring 10 m by 7 m by 3 m is completely filled with cubic boxes that have one metre long edges.

a) What is the volume of the room?

b) How many boxes are in the room?

c) If all the boxes were taken out of the room and put into a straight line, then how long would the line be?

6) Calculate the area:

a)

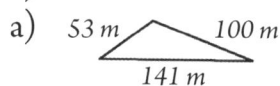
53 m — 100 m
141 m

b)

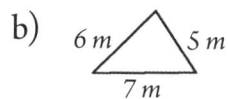
6 m — 5 m
7 m

7) *Challenge*
A conical drinking glass is 12 cm deep and 10 cm across at the top. If it is filled halfway to the top, then how full is it? Give your answer as a fraction (e.g. ½ full, ⅓ full, etc.).

Percents and Growth – Sheet 1a

Do 1 to 6 in your head. (Do you still remember all of your fraction to percent conversions?)

1) Convert to a percent:

a) $\frac{1}{2}$

b) $\frac{1}{3}$

c) $\frac{2}{3}$

d) $\frac{1}{4}$

e) $\frac{3}{4}$

f) $\frac{1}{5}$

g) $\frac{2}{5}$

h) $\frac{3}{5}$

i) $\frac{4}{5}$

j) $\frac{1}{6}$

k) $\frac{5}{6}$

l) $\frac{1}{8}$

m) $\frac{3}{8}$

n) $\frac{5}{8}$

o) $\frac{7}{8}$

2) Convert to a percent:
a) 0.23

b) 0.79

c) 0.04

d) 0.078

e) 0.0005

f) 1.4

3) Convert to a fraction.
a) 80%

b) 66²/₃%

c) 19%

d) 87½%

4) Convert to a decimal:
a) 63%

b) 8%

c) 64.27%

5) What is:
a) 10% of 58,000?

b) 1% of 58,000?

c) 60% of 350?

d) 62½% of 48?

6) a) 6 is what percent of 12?

b) 6 is what percent of 18?

c) 140 is what percent of 350?

d) 27,000 is what percent of 72,000?

e) 73 is what percent of 7,300?

f) 73 is what percent of 73,000?

g) 300 is 25% of what number?

h) 7,000 is 33¹/₃% of what number?

Show your work on a separate sheet, if necessary.
7) a) What is 71% of 800?

b) What is 400% of £470?

c) What is 0.6% of £470?

d) 810 is what percent of 1,080?

e) 126° is what percent of the whole circle?

f) 153 is 18% of what number?

8) *Increase/decrease*
a) What is 400 increased by 39%?

b) What is 72,000 decreased by 12½%?

Percents and Growth – Sheet 1b

Note: All banking interest problems in this unit are based upon an annual percentage rate (APR) compounded annually (i.e. not compounded monthly, daily, etc.), and it is assumed that there is no activity (i.e. no deposits or withdrawals) during the stated period of time.

1) a) 450 is what proportion (as a fraction) of 500?

   b) 500 is what proportion (as a fraction) of 450?

   c) 450 is what percent of 500?

   d) 500 is what percent of 450?

   e) 500 is what percent more than 450?

2) a) 30 is what proportion (as a fraction) of 75?

   b) 75 is what proportion (as a fraction) of 30?

   c) 30 is what percent of 75?

   d) 75 is what percent of 30?

   e) 75 is what percent more than 30?

3) Reword each 'increase/decrease' or 'more than/less than' statement as a straight percent:
   Example: Frank's salary is 15% less than Bill's.
      Frank's salary is 85% of Bill's.
   Example: My rent was increased by 35%.
      My rent is now 135% of what it was.

   a) The population of Happytown increased by 20% in the last year.

   b) Jack is 38% taller than Fred.

   c) The price has been increased by 300%.

   d) Bill weighs 15% less than Henry.

   e) The price has been decreased by 70%.

4) Reword each straight percent statement as an 'increase/decrease' or 'more than/less than' statement:
   a) Lenny weighs 180% as much as Mike.

   b) The price is 60% of what it was.

   c) Carol biked 400% as far as Alex.

5) Joe put £200 into a savings account at 5% interest. What is his balance after three years?

6) Give the formula that calculates the balance (P) of an account given the interest rate (r), initial deposit (P_0), and the number of years (t). (Hint: The previous problem can be done by taking 105% of each year's ending balance.)

Percents and Growth – Sheet 2a

Do 1 to 5 in your head!

1) Convert to a percent:
a) ⅓

b) ¾

c) ⅖

d) ⅙

e) ⅝

f) 0.84

g) 0.03

h) 0.092

i) 0.002

j) 2.7

2) Convert to a fraction.
a) 25%

b) 60%

c) 83⅓%

d) 12½%

3) Convert to a decimal:
a) 92%

b) 7%

c) 3.06%

4) What is:
a) 10% of 673?

b) 1% of 8,643?

c) 25% of 36?

d) 37½% of 72,000?

5) a) 70 is what percent of 210?

b) 860 is what percent of 8,600?

c) 15 is what percent of 25?

d) 2,800 is what percent of 3,200?

e) 6.4 is what percent of 640?

f) 70 is 20% of what number?

g) 800 is 16⅔% of what number?

Show your work on a separate sheet, if necessary.

6) a) What is 6% of 973?

b) What is 250% of £60?

c) What is 2.7% of 80,000?

d) 13 is what percent of 18?

7) Hank is 105 cm and Bobby is 168 cm:
a) Hank is what percent of Bobby's height?

b) Bobby is what percent of Hank's height?

8) Frank borrowed £500 from a bank at 10% APR. What does he owe, in total, after 6 years?

9) Jeff is 30% taller than Matt.'
a) Reword the above statement as a straight percent statement.

b) How tall is Jeff if Matt is 1.60 m?

10) Sales at Ball's Toy Store decreased by 35% in the last month.
a) Reword the above statement as a straight percent statement.

b) What is this month's sales if last month's sales were £48,000?

Percents and Growth – Sheet 2b

Different ways to solve for the base
(for more difficult problems)
Example: Joe has 37.5% as much money as Kate. How much does Kate have if Joe has £12?

The decimal method: Thinking of 37.5% as a decimal, we can say that Joe has 0.375 times as much as Kate. We can then see that the opposite is also true: Kate has Joe's amount divided by 0.375. So our answer is 12 ÷ 0.375 = £32.

The fraction method: Thinking of 37.5% as a fraction, we can say that Joe has ⅜ as much

as Kate. So we know that the opposite is also true: Kate has ⅜ as much as Joe. So our answer is: 12 × ⅜ = £32.

The algebra method: (Use this method only if you're really stuck.) We use the formula $n = P \times B$, which says that a number (n) is a certain percentage (P) of a base (B). For this problem, n is 12, and P is 37.5/100, which is more easily expressed as ⅜ or as 0.375. This gives the equation: 12 = ⅜ × B or 12 = 0.375 × B Solving either equation gives us B = £32.

1) Write down as many possible ways as you can think of to arrive at the answer for this problem: Heather is 62½% as tall as Jennifer. How tall is Jennifer if Heather is 115 cm?

2) Beth is 25% taller than Abe. (It may help to reword this statement.)
a) How tall is Beth if Abe is exactly 150 cm tall?

b) How tall is Abe if Beth is exactly 150 cm tall?

3) Circletown's population is increasing by 250 people per year, which is linear growth. Squareville's population is increasing at a rate of 10% per year, which is exponential growth. If both towns start with 2,000 residents, then:
a) What is the population of Circletown at the end of each year over the next eight years?

b) What is the population of Squareville at the end of each year over the next eight years?

c) What observations can be made about how each of the two towns have grown?

4) Use the *Growth rate table* (at the back of the book, p. 92) to answer each of the following.
a) In the column labelled 1.07 and the row labeled 6, we see the value 1.50073. What does this mean?

b) How could the value 1.50073 have been calculated by hand?

c) How could the numbers given in 4a) be used to say something about a bank account?

d) If Squareville continues to grow at 10% per year, what will its population be after 25 years?

e) If a population grows at a rate of 8% per year, how long does it take for it to double? How long does it take to triple?

Percents and Growth – Sheet 3a

Where possible, do it in your head, otherwise show your work on a separate sheet.

1) What is:
a) 10% of 892?

b) 13% of 73?

c) $16\frac{2}{3}$% of 7,200?

d) 80% of 15?

e) 3.5% of 240?

f) 400 increased by 50%?

g) 150% of 400?

h) 6,000 decreased by 10%?

i) 90% of 6,000?

j) 36 decreased by 75%?

k) 25% of 36?

l) 65.7 increased by 300%?

m) 400% of 65.7?

2) a) 180 is what proportion (as a fraction) of 270?

b) 270 is what proportion of 180?

c) 180 is what percent of 270?

d) 270 is what percent of 180?

e) Going from 180 up to 270 is what percentage increase?

f) Going from 270 down to 180 is what percentage decrease?

3) a) 18,000 is what percent of 24,000?

b) 35 is what percent of 56?

c) 27 is what percent of 40?

d) 100 is what percent of 120?

e) Going from 240 to 300 is what percentage increase?

f) Going from 30 to 50 is what percentage increase?

g) Going from 400 to 160 is what percentage decrease?

h) Going from 16 to 14 is what percentage decrease?

i) 3,000 is $12\frac{1}{2}$% of what number?

j) 23 is 61% of what number?

Word problems

4) Susan currently charges £25/hr for tutoring, but plans on raising her rates by 22%. What will her new rates be?

5) A bike originally marked at £180 is on sale at a 25% discount. What do you have to pay if there is a 6% delivery charge?

6) Mary bought a house for £62,500 and sold it for £67,500. What was the percentage profit?

7) Mark bought a new car for £26,000 and sold it a year later for £18,200. What is the depreciation (loss) of the car's value, as a percentage?

8) A town's population is 132,500. If this is a 6% increase from last year, what was the population last year?

9) Use the *Growth rate table* (p. 92)to answer each of the following:
a) Mark put £700 into a savings account at 3% APR. What will his balance be after 15 years?

b) Blueville currently has a population of 3,000 and is growing at 5% per year. What will its population be after 10 years?

Percents and Growth – Sheet 3b

Use the Growth rate table to solve each problem (p. 92).
1) Ruth put £1,000 into a savings account at 3.5% APR. What will her balance be:
a) After 10 years?

b) After 20 years?

c) After 40 years?

d) After 80 years?

e) Looking at the above answers, circle the correct answer below.
If we double the amount of time that the money is in the bank, then the amount of interest earned:
   is less than doubled
   is exactly doubled
   is more than doubled

2) Karen puts £10 into an investment account and makes a 20% return annually. How much money will she have:
a) After 10 years?

b) After 40 years?

c) After 80 years?

3) A business is growing by 10% per year. It now has 100 customers. At this rate, how many customers will it have:
a) In 5 years?

b) In 10 years?

c) In 50 years?

d) About how long will it take for there to be five times as many customers?

4) A business is growing by 50% per year. It now has 100 customers. At this rate, how many customers will it have:
a) In 5 years?

b) In 10 years?

c) In 50 years?

d) About how long will it take for there to be five times as many customers?

5) The population of a country is currently about 100 million and is increasing by 2% per year. What will its population be:
a) In 10 years?

b) In 50 years?

c) In 100 years?

d) About how long will it take for the population to increase by 48%?

6) The population of a country is currently about 100 million and is increasing by 4% per year. What will its population be:
a) In 10 years?

b) In 50 years?

c) In 100 years?

d) About how long will it take for the population to increase by 48%?

7) Jeff has a credit card debt of $100. If he neglects paying off any of his account, and he is charged 10% APR, then how much will his debt be:
a) After 5 years?

b) After 10 years?

c) After 50 years?

8) Use the *rule of 72* to quickly answer each.
a) How long does it take for your money to double in a savings account at 2% APR?

b) If a town doubles its population in 20 years, what is the average annual growth rate?

9) Use a calculator to calculate each as quickly as possible. Write down what you typed into your calculator.

a) 3,850 up to 4,543 is what percentage increase?

b) 584 up to 803 is what percentage increase?

c) 36,580 down to 34,751 is what percentage decrease?

Percents and Growth – Sheet 4

1) Use the *Growth rate table* (p. 92).
a) Annie put £100 into a savings account that earns 3% APR. What will the balance of the account be after 20 years?

b) The population of a city is about 100,000, and is increasing by 2.5% per year. Approximately, what will its population be in 50 years, if that growth rate continues?

c) The value of a certain stock is currently increasing by 30% annually. If it now is valued at £40 per share, then about how much will it be worth after 12 years, if that growth rate continues?

2) Use the *rule of 72* to quickly answer each:
a) How long does it take for your money to double at a return rate on your investment of 7% per year?

b) The price of properties in Clifton doubled over an eight-year period. What was the average annual growth rate over that period?

You may use a calculator for the rest of this sheet. You must write down what you put into your calculator. As always, round your answer to three significant digits, when necessary.

3) What is:
a) 7% of 89.3?

b) 1.3% of 730?

c) 0.04% of 34,200?

d) 320% of 45?

e) 458 increased by 12%?

f) 6,700 decreased by 60%?

4) 18 is what percent:
a) of 37?

b) of 370?

c) of 3,700?

d) of 5?

5) What percentage increase is it going from:
a) 480 up to 552?

b) 3,500 up to 3,654?

c) 65 up to 150?

6) What percentage decrease is it going from:
a) 420 down to 357?

b) 63,500 down to 12,700?

7) a) 456 is 38% of what?

b) 456 is 2.4% of what?

c) 72 is 60% more than what?

d) 9 is 7.1% more than what?

e) 770 is 12% less than what?

Word problems

8) A bike normally listed for £320 is on sale for a 30% discount. What is the new discounted price?

9) Kate bought a house for £198,000 and then sold it for £230,000 one year later. What is the profit as a percentage?

10) Fred bought a house for £230,000 and then sold it for £198,000 one year later. What is the loss as a percentage?

11) Ed is 64% as tall as Joe.
   a) How tall is Ed if Joe is 120 cm tall?

   b) How tall is Joe if Ed is 120 cm tall?

12) Tom is 8% taller than Pat.
   a) How tall is Tom if Pat is 135 cm tall?

   b) How tall is Pat if Tom is 135 cm tall?

13) A bank account increases by 7% per year for 5 years. What is the percentage increase over the 5-year period?

Percents and Growth – Sheet 5

Note: You may use a calculator for this sheet, but write down what goes into your calculator.

Solve each problem by using the *exponential growth formula*:

$$P = P_0(1+r)^t$$

Example: Annie puts £100 into a savings account that earns 3% APR. What will the balance of the account be after 20 years?

P_0 (initial amount) is 100; r (rate) is 0.03; and t (years) is 20. So we put $100 \times 1.03 \,\char`\^\, 20$ into the above formula and with a calculator we get £180.61.

(*Note:* The exponent key may be y^x or ^, depending on the calculator.)

1) The enrolment of a college is increasing by 15% per year. If the enrollment is currently about 3,000, what will it be after 18 years if that growth rate continues?

2) The population of a city is about 58,000, and is increasing by 5.6% per year. What will its population be in 10 years, if that growth rate continues?

Use the *rule of 72* to quickly answer each question.

3) Kim's investment doubled over a ten-year period. What was her average annual rate of return during this period?

4) The population of a country is growing at 1.2% per year. About how long will it take the population to double?

Mixed problems

5) What is 0.41% of 4,390?

6) What is 950 increased by 75%?

7) What is 175% of 950?

8) 37 is what percent of 51?

9) What percentage increase is it going from 6,200 up to 8,866?

10) 71.4 is 21% of what?

11) 992 is 55% more than what?

12) What is 72 decreased by 6%?

13) What percentage increase is it going from 54 up to 63?

14) What percentage decrease is it going from 61 down to 18.3?

15) 24 is what percent of 2,000?

16) 24 is what percent of 200?

17) 24 is what percent of 20?

18) What percentage increase is it going from 120 up to 300?

19) 5,727 is 17% less than what?

20) 74,200 is 1.4% of what?

21) What percentage decrease is it going from 83 down to 75.53?

22) 89 is 2.8% more than what?

23) What do you end up at when 400 is increased by 30% and then that result is decreased by 30%?

Word problems

24) Jim makes an 8.2% commission when he sells a car. How much does he earn by selling a £23,000 car?

25) Jill left a £6.00 tip, which was 8% of the meal's price. What was the price of the meal?

26) A bank account has an interest rate of 6% APR. What is the percentage increase of the balance over an 8-year period?

27) A sweater is marked at a discounted price of £33. If this was a 45% discount, then what was the original price?

28) Ellen is 80% as old as Vince. How old is Ellen if Vince is 60?

29) Ellen is 80% as old as Vince. How old is Vince if Ellen is 60?

30) Kevin has 16% more money than Dan. How much does Dan have if Kevin has £21.75?

31) Kevin has 16% more money than Dan. How much does Kevin have if Dan has £21.75?

32) *Challenge*
Julie is 30 years old, which is 37½% younger than Gail. What percent older than Julie will Gail be 12 years from now?

Percents and Growth – Sheet 6

Note: You may use a calculator for this sheet, but write down what goes into your calculator.

Mixed problems

1) What is 230 increased by 2.8%?

2) 53 is what percent of 66?

3) What percentage increase is it going from 17 up to 41?

4) 76.26 is 23% more than what?

5) 162 is 3.6% of what?

6) What percentage decrease is it going from 395 down to 158?

7) What is 8,200 decreased by 93%?

8) 69 is 11% less than what?

9) What is 265% of 4,300?

10) What is 4,300 increased by 165%?

11) 8 is what percent of 53?

12) 8 is what percent of 530?

13) What percentage increase is it going from 536 up to 737?

14) 6,794 is 79% of what?

15) 61.56 is 62% more than what?

16) What percentage decrease is it going from 320 down to 307.2?

17) What is 400 increased by 25%, and then decreased by 25%?

Use the rule of 72 *to quickly answer each.*

18) David's savings account earns 2.4% APR. How long does it take for his money to double?

19) Pam's house doubled in value over an 18-year period. What was the average annual rate at which the value was increasing during that period?

Word problems

20) Joan was billed £572.94 for a pair of skis. What was the marked price if there was a 6.1% surcharge for next day delivery?

21) Jen is 185 cm tall and her son Robbie is 74 cm tall.
   a) Robbie is what percent of Jen's height?

   b) Jen is what percent of Robbie's height?

   c) Robbie is what percent shorter than Jen?

   d) Jen is what percent taller than Robbie?

22) Bob weighs 20% more than Pete. If Pete weighs 80 kg:
   a) How much does Bob weigh?

   b) Pete weighs what percent less than Bob?

23) Mike weighs 20% less than Tom. If Mike weighs 90 kg:
   a) How much does Tom weigh?

   b) Tom weighs what percent more than Mike?

24) John has 35% as much money as Dave. How much does Dave have if John has £252?

25) In the year 2000, Japan had a population of 127 million with a 0.23% growth rate, and Nigeria had a population of 123 million with a 2.6% growth rate. Assuming that those growth rates continue:
   a) What was Japan's population in 2010?

   b) What will Japan's population be in 2080?

   c) What was Nigeria's population in 2010?

   d) What will Nigeria's population be in 2080?

   e) What can be said about the last answer?

26) *Challenge*
Depreciation is when the value of something drops. (e.g. The depreciation of a car is typically 30% in the first year.)

Sally bought a used car for £12,000 and it depreciated at a rate of 15% annually. How much was it worth after eight years?

Proportions – Sheet 1a

This whole unit contains a lot of questions in imperial units and later sheets have conversion between metric and imperial units.

Note: Throughout this whole unit you should:
(1) use the conversion tables at the back;
(2) use a calculator;
(3) write down what goes into your calculator;
(4) round your answers to three significant digits, when necessary.

1) John earns £52.40 in an 8-hour day. What is his hourly wage?

2) At an hourly wage of £8.35 per hour, how much does a worker make:
a) in an 8-hour day?

b) in a 40-hour week?

c) in a 50-week year?

3) Gail biked 110 km in four hours. What was her average speed?

4) How long does it take to fly 3,000 miles at a speed of 425 mph?

5) Ed biked the first 30 km of his bike trip in 2 hours and the remaining 40 km in 3 hours. What was his average speed for the whole trip?

6) *Measurement review*
a) 32 yds = _____ in

b) 0.07 mℓ = _____ ℓ

c) 0.375 lb = _____ oz

d) 72 in = _____ ft

e) 33,600 oz = _____ st

f) 3 pt = _____ fl oz

g) 3½ gal = _____ pt

h) 720 in = _____ yd

Proportion problems

A new way to solve ratio problems.

Example: Find x given that the two triangles below are similar.

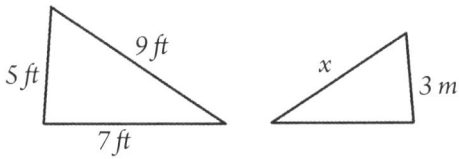

We set up a proportion in terms of long : short = long : short.

$$x : 3 = 9 : 5 \rightarrow \frac{x}{3} = \frac{9}{5}$$

By moving along diagonals we get:

$$x = \frac{3 \times 9}{5}$$

giving an answer of $5\frac{2}{5}$.

Example: A recipe calls for 600 mℓ of flour and 400 mℓ of water. How much water is needed if the recipe is expanded and 1,000 mℓ of flour are used?

We set up a proportion in terms of flour : water = flour : water.

$$600 : 400 = 1000 : x \rightarrow \frac{600}{400} = \frac{1000}{x}$$

By moving along diagonals we get:

$$x = \frac{1000 \times 400}{600} \text{ for an answer of } 666\frac{2}{3} \text{ mℓ.}$$

7) Find x given that these two triangles are similar.

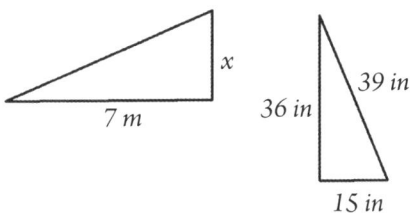

8) If 80 mℓ of rice require 180 mℓ of water, then how much water is needed for 150 mℓ of rice?

9) If it takes 39 gallons of fuel to drive 1,430 miles, then how many gallons are needed to drive 800 miles?

10) In Harry's class there are 18 boys and 24 girls.
 a) What is the ratio of boys to girls?

 b) Mary's class has the same ratio of boys to girls. If there are 15 boys, how many girls are there?

11) The ratio of cows to goats on a farm is 5 : 2. If the combined number of goats and cows is 119, then how many goats are there?

12) The map below has a (verbal) scale of 1 in = 300 miles. What is the distance, in reality, between the two locations marked on this map?

13) The true distance between two cities is 450 miles, but on a map it measures 3 inches. What is the (verbal) scale of the map?

Proportions – Sheet 1b

Two methods for converting units

Example: How many fl oz are in 5.2 litres?

Using the intuitive approach: If there is nothing on the conversion table that tells us how to go directly from litres to fluid ounces, we need to do the problem in two steps. One possibility is to first convert from litres to pints, and then from pints to fluid ounces. In converting from litres to pints, we know that one litre is about 1.76 pints. We then ask ourselves whether we should multiply 5.2 by 1.76, or divide 5.2 by 1.76. Only multiplying gives a reasonable answer. Therefore, 5.2 ℓ is 5.2 × 1.76 = 9.152 pt.

Now, in converting to fl oz, we know that 1 pint is 20 fl oz. We ask ourselves whether to multiply 9.152 by 20 or divide 9.152 by 20. Only multiplying gives a reasonable answer. Therefore, our final answer is: 9.152 × 20 = 183 fl oz.

Solution using the chain method: Usually, we only need to use the chain method for more complicated problems, or if we are really stuck. This method focuses on getting units to cancel until only the desired unit is left. Mathematically speaking, we are multiplying our original amount by fractions that are equal to one – in other words, where the numerators and denominators are equal. The work looks like this:

$$\frac{5.2\ell}{1} \times \frac{1.76\,\text{pt}}{1\ell} \times \frac{20\,\text{fl oz}}{1\,\text{pt}}$$

Notice that all the units cross cancel, except for 'fl oz'. On our calculator we do 5.2 × 1.76 × 20, giving an answer of 183 fl oz.

1) *Conversion problems*
a) 29 lb ≈ _____ kg

b) 300 mℓ ≈ _____ fl oz

c) 18 mi ≈ _____ km

d) 9.2 ℓ ≈ _____ gal

e) 32 in ≈ _____ mm

f) 0.76 km ≈ _____ yd

g) 5 ft 8 in ≈ _____ m

h) 1.7 tonnes ≈ _____ lb.

2) The length of a running course is carefully measured both as 1,250 m and 4,104 ft. Without using the conversion table, answer the following. Show your work.

a) How many feet are in one metre?

b) How many metres are in one foot?

c) Check your answers for the above questions by looking in the conversion table (p. 93). What is the relationship between the two numbers given as answers for parts a) and b)?

3) *Reciprocals.* For each problem, calculate the answer, then afterwards, check your answer (for the harder ones) by looking in the conversion table.
a) 1 yd = 3 ft → 1 ft = _____ yd

b) 1 gal = 8 pt → 1 pt = _____ gal

c) 1 cm = 0.01 m → 1 m = _____ cm

d) 1 mi ≈ 1.6093 km → 1 km ≈ _____ mi

e) 1 kg ≈ 2.2046 lb → 1 lb ≈ _____ kg

f) 1 ℓ ≈ 1.76 pt → 1 pt ≈ _____ ℓ

A Student's Workbook for Mathematics in Class 8

g) 1 ft ≈ 0.3048 m → 1 m ≈ _____ ft

h) 1 in ≈ 2.54 cm → 1 cm ≈ _____ in

4) Opposite is a map of Eagle Island. The scale is 1 inch = 2.4 miles. There is a bike path that goes straight across the island, connecting the two furthest apart points.

a) How long is the bike path?

b) How long would it take (to the nearest minute) to bike across the island if you averaged 13 mph?

c) What is the fractional scale of the map?

Proportions – Sheet 2a

1) At a restaurant, 40 loaves of bread are needed to serve 136 guests. How many (whole) loaves of bread are needed to serve 90 guests?

2) A recipe calls for 300 mℓ of water and 500 mℓ of flour. How much water is needed if the recipe is expanded and 800 mℓ of flour are used?

3) At Jan's school, the ratio of tennis players to basketball players is 4 : 7. How many tennis players are there if there are 84 basketball players?

4) A 2,000-mile flight from Denver to Boston takes 3 hours and 45 minutes. What is the average speed of the plane?

5) Write the four ways to express the ratio of this rectangle's dimensions.

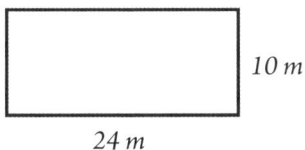

[rectangle labeled 10 m on right side and 24 m on bottom]

6) What is the average speed of a cyclist who goes up a 10-mile hill in 3 hours and 25 minutes, and then comes down in just 20 minutes?

7) Jill drove 348 km and used 23.0 ℓ of petrol.
a) What was her car's fuel efficiency in ℓ/100 km?

b) At that rate of fuel consumption, how far can she go on 53 ℓ of petrol?

c) At that rate of fuel consumption, how much petrol is required to go 187 km?

8) 682 cm = _____ km

9) 1.8 km = _____ cm

10) 4½ lb = _____ oz

11) 2.6 mi = _____ ft

12) 2.6 mi = _____ yd

13) 160 fl oz = _____ pt

14) 63 m ≈ _____ ft

15) 63 ft ≈ _____ m

16) 200 km ≈ _____ mi

17) 200 mi ≈ _____ km

18) 153 lb ≈ _____ kg

19) 153 kg ≈ _____ lb

20) 9.3 gal ≈ _____ ℓ

21) 9.3 ℓ ≈ _____ gal

22) 16 ft ≈ _____ cm

23) 3.2 ℓ ≈ _____ pt

24) A map of Poland has a (fractional) scale of 1 : 750 000.
 a) What does the scale mean?

 b) The distance from Krakow to Warsaw measures 33 cm on the map. What is the true distance between the cities?

25) The Sears Tower in Chicago has a height of 1,452 ft, not including the antennae at the top. Give both types of scales of the drawing of the Sears Tower, shown here.

26) The distance from Clifton to Borgen is 128 km, or 79 miles.

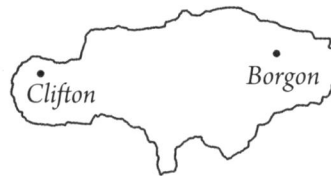

 a) What is the verbal scale in the metric system?

 b) What is the verbal scale in imperial units?

 c) What is the fractional scale?

Proportions – Sheet 2b

1) A recipe calls for 300 mℓ of flour and makes 8 servings. How much flour is required in order to enlarge the recipe to make 21 servings (to the nearest 10 mℓ)?

2) The ratio of adults to children at a fair is 4 : 9. How many adults are there if there are 207 children?

3) A group of 40 people had to pay £110 for admission to a museum. What would the cost be for a group of 16 people?

4) A farmer figures that planting 90 hectares will produce 225 m³ of wheat. How many hectares should be planted in order to produce 500 m³ of wheat?

5) A recipe calls for 750 g of flour to make two dozen muffins. How much flour is needed to make 40 muffins?

6) Bill walks at a rate of 3 mph for 4 hours, then bikes for 2 hours at 12 mph. What is the average speed for the trip?

7) Lori's car uses 40.5 ℓ of petrol to go 485 km. At that rate of fuel consumption:
a) How far can she go on 30 ℓ of petrol?

b) How many litres are needed for a 1,150-km trip?

8) What is the greatest distance between two points of the island given that the scale of the map below is 1 : 10 000?

9) A map has a scale of 1 inch = 80 miles. What distance on the map represents 350 miles?

10) On a map, the distance between two cities is 3.4 cm. In reality, they are 680 km apart. Give both types of scales for the map.

11) It takes Mary and Harry an average of 9 days to paint four houses.
a) How long does it take them to paint 12 houses?

b) How many houses can they paint in 30 days?

c) How long does it take them to paint 23 houses?

12) *Unit conversions*
a) 100 g ≈ _____ oz

b) 20 fl oz ≈ _____ mℓ

c) 4.3 ℓ ≈ _____ fl oz

d) 2½ pt ≈ _____ ℓ

e) 27 m ≈ _____ ft

f) 9½ in ≈ _____ cm

g) 782 km ≈ _____ mi

13) A car has a petrol tank that holds 50 ℓ. How many gallons is that?

14) Alex can type 500 words in 8 minutes.
a) How long does it take him to type 2,100 words?

b) How many words can he type in an hour?

15) A cylindrical bucket has a 1 foot diameter and an 18 inch height. Calculate its capacity, both in litres and in gallons (given that 1 gal ≈ 277 in³).

16) *Challenge*
After a heavy snowfall, Bill starts shovelling his driveway, which is 60 m long, at 10:50. At 11:30 he has done the first 25 m. At what time will he finish?

Proportions – Sheet 3a

Tips for density problems
- Density is weight per volume.
- The main density formula is: $D = \frac{W}{V}$

To solve some of the problems you need to look up the density in the conversion table at the end of the book (p. 93).

1) Calculate the density of a block:
a) That weighs 8 g and has a volume of 16 cm³.

b) That weighs 60 g and has a volume of 80 cm³.

c) That weighs 130 kg and has a volume of 0.23 m³.

d) That weighs 158 lb and has a volume of 3.7 ft³.

e) Which of the above blocks float in water?

2) How much does a cube of iron weigh that has 8-inch long edges?

3) 63 grams of mercury has a volume of how many millilitres?

4) A cylindrical bucket has both a diameter and a height of 10 inches.
a) What is the volume of the bucket, both in cubic inches and in cubic cm?

b) If the bucket is filled with water, what is the weight of the water, both in lb and in kg?

c) If the bucket is filled with mercury, what is the weight of the mercury, both in lb and in kg?

5) If necessary, use the *chain method* to solve each problem. Show your work.
a) Length: 528 mm ≈ _____ ft

b) Volume. 3.29 ℓ ≈ _____ fl oz

c) Speed: 7.2 yd/sec ≈ _____ km/h

d) Density: 1,204 lb/ft³ ≈ _____ kg/m³

6) *Challenge: the grains of rice problem*
A wise man was granted a request. He requested that a single grain of rice be placed on the first square of a chess board, 2 grains on the second square, 4 grains on the third, 8 grains on the fourth and so on, doubling with every square up until the last square – the 64th square.

a) How many grains of rice are there on the whole chessboard (assuming that it would somehow fit)?

b) How many sacks of rice would this be, and if all the sacks were laid in a line end-to-end, how far would they stretch? (Assume that each sack is 50 cm long and contains around 400,000 grains of rice.)

c) What is the volume of the rice? (Assume that there are 30 grains of rice in a mℓ.)

Proportions – Sheet 3b

1) Find the fractional scale of a map that has a verbal scale of:
a) 1 inch = 0.375 miles.

b) 1 cm = 0.4 km.

2) A map has a fractional scale of 1 : 50,000.
a) What distance on the map represents 15 km?
b) This map is most likely which of the following:
   A walking map of national park
   A driving map of a wider region
   A map of a country

3) There are two maps of Japan on the wall of a classroom. The one next to the door has a scale of 1 : 2,000,000, and the one next to the window has a scale of 1 : 5,000,000. Which map is larger?

4) On a 300 g package of rice, the directions say to make 5 servings add 800 mℓ of water. How much rice and water are needed for 12 servings?

5) Phil can paint 3 chairs in 1 hour and 40 minutes.
a) How long does it take him to paint 20 chairs?

b) How many chairs can he paint in a 40-hour workweek?

The intuitive approach
6) a) One hour is how many minutes?

b) How do you convert km/min into km/h?

c) 3 km/min = _____ km/h

7) a) How many metres are in one km?

b) How do you convert m/h into km/h?

c) 6,700 m/h = _____ km/h

8) a) One hour is how many seconds?

b) How do you convert m/s into m/h?

c) 8.3 m/s = _____ m/h

9) a) How do you convert m/s into km/h?

b) 23 m/s = _____ km/h

10) a) How do you convert km/h into m/s?

b) 45 km/h = _____ m/s

11) a) How do you convert ft/sec into mph?

b) 14.8 ft/sec ≈ _____ mph

Unit conversions

12) 8.8 lb ≈ _____ kg

13) 8.8 kg ≈ _____ lb

14) 20 mm ≈ _____ ft

15) 7,800 mℓ ≈ _____ pt

16) 36 km/h = _____ km/min

17) 42 km/h = _____ m/h

18) 5 mi/min = _____ mph

19) 30 mph ≈ _____ km/hr

20) 36 km/h = _____ m/s

21) How much does a block of solid gold weigh that is 10 cm × 12 cm × 24 cm (the size of a tissue box)?

22) On a certain day there were following exchange rates:
US dollar: $1.43/£
Euro: €1.28/£
Japan yen: ¥150/£

a) A quarter US dollar is worth about the same as which British coin?

b) Three yen is worth about the same as which British coin?

c) How much is one dollar, one euro and one yen in British currency?

23) Milk in the Britain costs £1.39/ℓ. Compare the milk prices given below by converting everything to £/ℓ. Use the *chain method*.

a) Japan: ¥207/ℓ

b) USA: $3.69/US gallon (1 US gallon is 3.785 ℓ)

Proportions – Sheet 4

Are there too many people in the world?

Note: You are not allowed to use the conversion table for this worksheet. Instead, the following estimates will help you:

- The diameter of the earth is 12,742 km.
- Approximately 70.8% of the earth is covered with water.
- Approximately 32% of the earth's land area is 'wasteland' (i.e. too rocky, dry, cold, or barren to grow anything). The rest we will consider to be 'fertile land' (i.e. farmland, pasture, forest).
- The Grand Canyon has a volume very close to 4,000 cubic km.
- An average person's arm span is about 145 cm.
- The world's population is roughly 7 billion.
- 100 hectares (ha) = 1 km².

1) *One-dimensional.* If all the people in the world were to join hands to form a line, then how long would that line be? How many times around the equator would this line of people stretch?

2) *Three-dimensional.* If we took all the people in the world, and put each person in a box that has a floor area of 200 m² and 2.5 m high ceilings, then what would be the volume of all these boxes added together? How many times bigger than the volume of the Grand Canyon would this be?

3) *Two-dimensional.* How many ha of 'fertile land' are there per household? (Assume that everyone is in a four-person household.)

Proportions – Sheet 5

1) *Unit conversions*

   a) 400 yd ≈ _____ km

   b) 3 pt ≈ _____ mℓ

   c) 50 g ≈ _____ oz

   d) 780 cm ≈ _____ ft

   e) 3 ft 9 in ≈ _____ mm

   f) 12 m/s = _____ km/h

   g) 40 mph ≈ _____ m/s

   h) 10 ft/sec = _____ mph

2) Calculate the following. Use the conversion table (p. 93) only to check your answer. (Hint: 1 in ≈ 2.54 cm, 1 m ≈ 3.28 ft)

   a) $1 \text{ ft}^2 =$ _____ in^2

   b) $1 \text{ m}^2 =$ _____ cm^2

   c) $1 \text{ in}^2 \approx$ _____ cm^2

   d) $1 \text{ cm}^2 \approx$ _____ in^2

   e) $1 \text{ m}^2 \approx$ _____ ft^2

   f) $1 \text{ ft}^2 \approx$ _____ m^2

   g) $1 \text{ in}^3 \approx$ _____ cm^3

   h) $1 \text{ m}^3 \approx$ _____ ft^3

3) Use following exchange rates, and use the chain method, if necessary.
   US dollar: $1.43/£
   Euro: €1.28/£
   Japan yen: ¥150/£

   a) $600 = £ _____

   b) ¥8,560 = £ _____

   c) £80 = ¥_____

   d) ¥1,000,000 = £ _____

   e) €50 = £ _____

   f) £50 = €_____

   g) ¥50,000 = $ _____

   h) €5,300 = ¥ _____

4) A machine can pump 500 ℓ of water in 25 minutes. How much can it pump in 3 hours?

5) Mary can tune-up 26 bikes in one 8-hour day.
   a) How many bikes can she tune-up in a 40-hour week?

   b) How many bikes can she completely tune-up in five hours?

   c) How long does it take her to tune-up 80 bikes?

6) Jane's car has a fuel efficiency of 34 mpg. What is this in km/ℓ?

7) Which is traveling faster, a plane flying at 720 km/h or one flying at 240 m/s?

8) The speed of light is approximately 186,000 mi/sec.
a) What is this in mph?

b) How far does light travel in 3 minutes?

9) A snail is moving at a rate of an inch every 20 seconds.

a) What is the speed of the snail in inches per second?

b) What is the speed of the snail in feet per hour?

c) What is the speed of the snail in miles per hour?

d) How far does the snail go in 45 minutes?

e) How long does it take the snail to go 27 feet?

10) What is the density (in g/cm^3) of a cube that weighs 1.6 kg and has edges that are 5.3 cm long?

11) A concrete block measures 30 cm by 15 cm by 20 cm. What does the block weigh (in kg) if the density of concrete is 2.1 g/cm^3?

12) What is the volume (in cm^3) of 3 kg of gold?

13) An empty container weighs 250 g and has a capacity of 1,750 cm^3. What is the total weight (in kg) of the container when it is filled:
a) with water?

b) with oil?
(The density of oil ≈ 0.87g/cm^3.)

c) with mercury?

Proportions – Sheet 6

1) *Unit conversions*

   a) $3.8 \, \text{lb} \approx$ _____ g

   b) $270 \, \text{cm} \approx$ _____ yd

   c) $3 \, \text{yd}^3 \approx$ _____ m^3

   d) $0.091 \, \text{oz} \approx$ _____ mg

   e) $830 \, \text{km}^2 \approx$ _____ mi^2

   f) $830 \, \text{mi}^2 \approx$ _____ km^2

   g) $7.8 \, \text{mi/min} \approx$ _____ m/s

   h) $58 \, \text{cm/s} \approx$ _____ mph

2) Use the chain method (don't use the conversion factors listed under *Density* in the conversion table):

   a) $1 \, \text{oz/in}^3 \approx$ _____ g/cm^3

   b) $1 \, \text{g/cm}^3 \approx$ _____ oz/in^3

3) The speed of sound is approximately 335 m/sec.
   a) If you see a strike of lightning and then 3 seconds later hear the thunder, about how far are you from the source of the lightning?

   b) Explain how you can estimate how far away a storm is by counting the seconds between seeing the lightning and hearing the thunder.

   c) What is the speed of sound in mph?

   d) How far (in km) does sound travel in 3 minutes?

4) On a certain date, petrol prices in Britain were £1.22/ℓ. Petrol prices from other countries are shown below. Compare prices by converting to pounds per litre (to the nearest penny) using the exchange rates below:
   US dollar: $1.43/£
   Euro: €1.28/£
   Japan yen: ¥150/£
   a) United States: 2.31/US gallon (which is 3.78 ℓ)

   b) Japan: ¥118/ℓ

   c) Ireland: €1.31/l

5) Kathy has determined that her woodstove requires 35 logs to keep her cabin warm for 24 hours.
   a) At this rate, how long will a pile of 400 logs last?

   b) How many logs will she need to heat her cabin for one week?

6) How much does a cube of solid gold weigh if it has edges that are 20 cm long?

7) What is the volume (in cm^3) of a block of aluminium that weighs 10 kg?

8) What is the density (in g/cm^3) of a ball that is 46 cm in diameter and weighs 9 kg? What percent as dense as water is it?

9) A block has a volume of 508 cm^3, and weighs 1.9 kg.
a) What is the density of the block (in g/cm^3)?

b) What is the density of the block (in lb/ft^3)?

c) What is the density of the block (in kg/m^3)?

d) What is the density of the block (in oz/in^3)?

e) What substance do you think the block is made of?

10) A small stone pyramid weighs 5.52 kg, has a height of 12 cm and has a square base with 20 cm-long sides.
a) What is its density (in g/cm^3)?

b) What does it weigh in water (in kg)?

Proportions – Sheet 7

1) *Unit conversions*

a) 7 lb ≈ _____ kg

b) 380 g ≈ _____ oz

c) 72 cm ≈ _____ in

d) 4½ pt ≈ _____ ml

e) 3.1 km ≈ _____ yd

f) 54 ft^3 = _____ in^3

g) 54 ft^3 = _____ yd^3

h) 54 ft^3 ≈ _____ m^3

i) 54 ft^3 ≈ _____ ℓ

j) 700 kg/m^3 = _____ g/cm^3

k) 2.8 g/cm^3 ≈ _____ lb/ft^3

l) 2.63 m/s = _____ km/h

m) 130 km/h ≈ _____ mph

2) The exchange rate for the Indian rupee is 97 rupees per pound.

a) 97 Rs/£ ≈ _____ £/Rs

b) £200 = _____ Rs

c) £3.39/imp gal ≈ _____ Rs/ℓ

3) Charlie's lawnmower uses 1¼ ℓ of petrol to mow ¾ of his lawn. How much petrol does it take to mow his whole lawn?

4) A road crew can pave 28 km of road in five 8-hour days.
a) How much road can they pave in 15 days?

b) How much road can they pave in 4 days?

c) How long does it take to pave 63 km of road?

5) Paul bikes up an 8-km hill averaging 8 km/h, and then bikes down the same hill at 32 km/h. What was his average speed for the whole trip?

6) A map has a fractional scale of 1 : 1 000 000.
a) Two towns on the map measure 6.3 cm apart. What is the real distance between the towns?

b) What is the verbal scale in metric?

c) What is the verbal scale in imperial measures?

7) A map of the Cotswolds in England has a distance of 54 cm between Stroud and Gloucester. The actual distance between these two places is 13.5 km. What are the two scales of the map?

8) If it takes 91 ℓ of pettrol to drive 1,090 km, how far can you drive on 64 ℓ?

9) A recipe calls for 50 mℓ of oil to make 4 enchiladas. How much oil is needed in order to make 30 enchiladas?

10) Alex can make 25 burritos in 40 minutes. How long does it take him to make 35 burritos?

11) A petrol tank in the shape of a rectangular prism (i.e. a box) measures 18 cm by 45 cm by 60 cm. Petrol has a density of about 660 kg/m³.
a) What is the capacity of the tank, in litres?

b) What is the capacity of the tank, in gallons?

c) What is the density of petrol, in lb/ft³?

d) How much does 5.3m³ of petrol weigh?

e) How much does a litre of petrol weigh?

f) How much does a gallon of petrol weigh (in lb)?

g) What is the weight of the petrol when the tank is full? (Give your answer both in kg and in lb)

12) What is the weight of a cubic km of air? (Assume a uniform density of $1.29 \, kg/m^3$)

Algebra – Sheet 1

Showing work

Throughout this unit, you should show each of the steps when solving an equation, even if you can do the problem easily in your head. Although it may not seem necessary, this will help you to develop the skills needed later for complex problems.

Formulas

1) *Galileo's law of falling bodies*
   $D = 4.9 \times T^2$
   where D is the number of metres an object falls (disregarding air resistance) after being dropped for T seconds. Calculate the distance that an object falls after being dropped:
   a) For 4 seconds.

   b) For 2½ seconds.

2) Use the temperature conversion formulas:
   $C = \frac{5}{9} \times (F - 32)$

   $F = \frac{9}{5} \times C + 32$

a) Convert 10°C to °F.

b) Convert −15°C to °F.

c) Convert 113°F to °C.

d) Convert 23°F to °C.

Signed numbers
Simplify:
3) −9 + 15

4) −9 − 15

5) 28 − 32

6) −32 + 28

7) (3)(7)

8) (3)(−7)

9) 3 − 7

10) $(-3)(+7)$

11) $-3 + 7$

12) $(-3)(-7)$

13) $-3 - 7$

14) $(-15) \div (-5)$

15) $(15) \div (-5)$

16) $\frac{15}{-5}$

17) $9 - (-4)$

18) $7 - (+11)$

19) $-3 - (-9)$

20) $-7 - (-2 - 8)$

Expressions

Simplify by combining like terms:

21) $5x + 7x$

22) $3a + 3x - 8a$

23) $2 + 5x - 7$

24) $3y - 4 + x - 12 - x + y$

25) $3x - 73 + 10x$

26) $-5x + 1 - 5x - 5$

27) $x - y - 3x + 6$

Equations

Solve each equation by getting x alone. Show what is done to each side.

Example:
$$\begin{array}{rcr} x + 12 & = & 7 \\ -12 & & -12 \\ \hline x & = & -5 \end{array}$$

28) $x - 1 = -7$

29) $5x = 35$

30) $35x = 5$

31) $x \div 4 = 12$

32) $x + 5 = -3$

33) $x \div 3 = -12$

34) $-2x = 14$

35) $7x - 3 = 4x + 18$

Algebra – Sheet 2

Formulas

1) Convert 59°F to °C.

2) Convert –5°C to °F.

3) Convert 70°F to °C.

4) Convert 42°C to °F.

5) Calculate the distance that an object falls after being dropped for 1½ seconds.

Signed numbers

Simplify:

6) $-2 + 7$

7) $-5 + 3$

8) $-5 - 3$

9) $(24) \div (-2)$

10) $(-24) \div (2)$

11) $\frac{-24}{2}$

12) $(-24) \div (-2)$

13) $\frac{-24}{-2}$

14) $13 - (-8)$

15) $7 - (+2)$

16) $7 + (-2)$

17) $-6 - (-2) + (-3) - (+4)$

Expressions

Simplify by combining like terms:

18) $x - 7 - 3x - 8$

19) $-3x - 7 + x - 9$

20) $-x - 2 - 6x + 8$

21) $-6 - 4 + 2 - 9 + 4$

22) $-2 + (-9) - (-4) - (+1)$

Order of operations

Simplify:

23) $5 + 3 \times 2$

24) $(5 + 3) \times 2$

25) $7 - 5 \times 3$

26) $(7 - 5) \times 3$

27) 4×5^2

28) $(4 \times 5)^2$

29) $8 + 20 \div 4$

Distributive property

Simplify:

30) $4(3x - 5)$

31) $3(x + 7)$

32) $-6(7x + 4)$

33) $-3(x - 4)$

Equations

Solve each equation by getting x alone. Show what is done to each side.

34) $x - 8 = 12$

35) $8x = 40$

36) $8x = -40$

37) $-8x = -40$

38) $-8 + x = 40$

39) $3x - 1 = 5x + 9$

40) $7x + 5 = 9x + 17$

41) $5x - 7 = -x + 3$

Algebra – Sheet 3

Signed numbers

Simplify:

1) $(-6)(-7)$

2) $-6 - 7$

3) $(-3)(8)$

4) $\frac{-30}{-6}$

5) $\frac{30}{-6}$

6) $\frac{-30}{6}$

7) $5 + (-9)$

8) $-15 - (-5)$

9) $-2 - (+9) - (-7) - (+4)$

Order of operations

Simplify:

10) $10 - 7 \times 2$

11) $8 \times 2 + 6 \div 4$

12) $18 \div 12 \div 4$

13) $7 - 4 \times 2^3 + 50$

Laws of exponents

Fill-in the boxes with an exponent or co-efficient:

14) $3^2 \times 3^4 \rightarrow 3^{\square}$

15) $5^3 \times 5^7 \rightarrow 5^{\square}$

16) $x^4 \times x^5 \rightarrow x^{\square}$

17) $(3^2)^4 \rightarrow 3^{\square}$

18) $(7^3)^3 \rightarrow 7^{\square}$

19) $(x^5)^2 \rightarrow x^{\square}$

20) $3x^3 + 5x^3 \rightarrow \square x^{\square}$

21) $8x^4 - 6x^4 \rightarrow \square x^{\square}$

Distributive property
Simplify:

22) $5(3x + 2)$

23) $-3(4x - 5)$

24) $5 + 3(x - 7)$

25) $7 - 2(4x + 3) + x$

Equations
Solve each equation by getting x alone. Show what is done to each side.

26) $-4x = 28$

27) $-3x = -21$

28) $x + 6 = -10$

29) $x - 6 = 10$

30) $x \div 3 = 21$

31) $\frac{x}{3} = 21$

32) $\frac{1}{3}x = 21$

33) $\frac{1}{3} + x = 21$

34) $-12x = -4$

35) $\frac{3}{5}x = \frac{4}{5}$

36) $\frac{3}{5} + x = \frac{4}{5}$

37) $\frac{-5}{12}x = \frac{5}{8}$

38) $2(2x + 9) = 4$

39) $-7x + 35 = -2x$

40) $6x - 7 = 8 - 3(x - 4)$

41) $1\frac{1}{3}x - 3 = 5x + 4\frac{1}{2}$

Algebra – Sheet 4

Simplify:

1) $x + x + y + y$

2) $7x - f + x - b - f$

3) $-3x - 7 - x + 9$

4) $-8 - 2 + 6 - 7 + 4$

5) $-5 + (-9) - (+7) - (-2)$

6) $(-4)^2$

7) $(-4)^3$

8) $(-4)^4$

9) $30 \div 8 \div 4$

10) $10 - 8 \times 10^3 \div 4 \times 2$

11) $8(3x + 5)$

12) $-4(2x - 7)$

13) $6 - 3(2x - 5) + 8x$

14) $x^3 \times x^4$

15) $y^2 \times y^5$

16) $(x^2)^3$

17) $7x^2 + 4x^2$

18) $8x^5 - 3x^2$

19) $2^5 \times 2^3$ equals
    (a) 2^{15} (b) 2^8 (c) 4^8

20) $2^5 \times 3^4$ equals
    (a) 6^{20} (b) 6^9 (c) neither

21) $(9^4)^2$ equals
    (a) 9^8 (b) 9^{16} (c) neither

22) Which fraction isn't equal to the others?
    (a) $\frac{3}{-7}$ (b) $\frac{-3}{7}$ (c) $\frac{-3}{-7}$ (d) $-\frac{3}{7}$

Evaluate each expression given $x = 3$; $y = -4$;
    $z = -10$

23) $x^2 + 2y + 3z$

24) $y^2 - 5z$

25) $7x + 5yz - 3z$

Solve each equation:

26) $-5x = -30$

27) $x + 10 = -2$

28) $-x - 5 = -1$

29) $-6x + 3 = -15$

30) $\frac{x}{5} = -8$

31) $\frac{3}{5}x = \frac{9}{10}$

32) $\frac{3}{5} - x = \frac{9}{10}$

33) $4x = \frac{2}{5}$

34) $\frac{8}{9} = \frac{12}{x}$

35) $\frac{8}{15x} = \frac{12}{5}$

36) $\frac{4}{x} = \frac{9}{x-5}$

37) $7x - 67 = -3x - 7$

38) $-2x - 11 = 9x - 3$

39) $4x - 8 - 6x = -7 - 3x - 3$

40) $4x + 2(x - 3) = 10 - 6(3x + 4)$

Algebra – Sheet 5

Simplify:
1) $24 \div 3 + 9 \times 2$

2) $7 - 3 \times 2^3$

3) $6 + 36 \div 6 + 2 \times 2^2$

4) $9 - 7(8 - 5 \times 2)^2 - 5$

5) $9(317 - 320) - 8$

6) $9(3x - 4) - 3$

7) $x^6 \times x^3$

8) $a^3 \times a^5$

9) $(x^6)^2$

10) $3x^5 + 7x^5$

11) $6x^3 - x^3$

12) $6x^3 + 4x^2$

Evaluate each expression given that $x = -1$; $y = 0$; $z = 5$.
13) $z^3 - 4xz^2$

14) $7x^2y^3z^4$

15) $x^9 + 23y^5 - 6z$

Solve each equation:
16) $8 - x = 12$

17) $-6x = -24$

18) $-12x = 4$

19) $-1\frac{3}{5}x = \frac{4}{7}$

20) $-5x = -7\frac{1}{7}$

21) $2x - \frac{3}{4} = -3$

22) $\frac{-5}{3} = \frac{-4}{3x}$

23) $5x - 4 = 2x + 23$

24) $\frac{3}{x+5} = \frac{-4}{2x-5}$

25) $19 - 3(2x - 7) + 5x = 3x + 4(x - 8)$

26) $-\frac{1}{6}x + \frac{2}{3} - \frac{3}{4}x = \frac{7}{10} + \frac{2}{3}x - \frac{2}{5}$

27) $44x - 7 - 4(3x + 5) + 5 - 3(4x - 2) - 6$
$= 3x - 5x + 30 + 9(x - 2) - 8$

Algebra – Sheet 6

Simplify:

1) $4 + 3 \times 9$

2) $6 - 5 \times 3 + 20$

3) $7 \times 3 + 12 \div (9 - 10)$

4) $30 - 10 \times 3^2$

5) $c^4 \times c^5$

6) $c^3 \times x^2$

7) $x^2 \times x^5$

8) $(x^2)^5$

9) $(x^5)^2$

10) $5x^7 + 8x^7$

11) $x^3 - 5x^3$

12) $5x^4 + 3x^3$

Evaluate each expression given that $x = 3$; $y = -4$.

13) $5y - 6x + 3$

14) $y^2 - xy + 4$

Solve each equation:

15) $6x = -\frac{4}{5}$

16) $-8x = -3$

17) $-2\frac{2}{3}x = -\frac{4}{7}$

18) $2\frac{2}{3} - x = -\frac{4}{7}$

19) $-6x - 11 = -x - 14$

20) $\frac{-5}{3x + 1} = \frac{2}{2x - 3}$

21) $-8x + 3 - 5x = 7 + 2(x - 7)$

22) $\frac{2}{9}\left(3x - \frac{1}{2}\right) = \frac{1}{5}x + \frac{1}{3}$

23) $\frac{3}{5} + \frac{1}{2}(3x - 1) = \frac{2}{5}\left(\frac{3}{2}x - 2\right) - 1\frac{1}{2}$

24) $8 + 2(3x - 4) - 3x - 4(x + 7) =$
     $5 - 3(x - 6) + 3x + 8(3 - 2x)$

25) *Challenge*

     $\frac{2}{5}x - 8\frac{1}{8} - \frac{3}{4}\left(\frac{14}{15}x - 5\frac{5}{9}\right)$
     $= \frac{27}{10}x - 2\frac{5}{6} + \frac{3}{4}\left(x + 5\frac{1}{6}\right)$

End of Year Review – Sheet 1

1) Using this triangle:

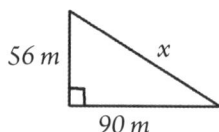

56 m, x, 90 m

a) Find x by using Pythagorean triples.

b) Calculate the area.

2) Use the square root algorithm to calculate $\sqrt{71}$ (rounded to three significant digits).

3) A triangle has three sides measuring 60 cm, 70 cm and 90 cm. Is it an acute, an obtuse or a right triangle?

4) Calculate the volume of a sphere with a 10 cm radius.

5) Calculate the volume and surface area of a box that measures 3 by 4 by 5 cm.

6) a) How many mm^2 are in a cm^2?

b) How many mm^3 are in a cm^3?

7) What is 13% of 350?

8) 60 is what percent of 75?

9) 75 is what percent of 60?

10) What percentage increase is it going from 360 up to 420?

11) 123 is 64% more than what?

12) What is 620 decreased by 9%?

13) Fred put £6,000 into a savings account that earns 2% APR. What will the balance of the account be after 30 years?

14) If a town doubles its population in 35 years, then what, approximately, is the average annual growth rate?

15) Joe is 85% as tall as Rick.
a) How tall is Joe if Rick is 153 cm tall?

b) How tall is Rick if Joe is 153 cm tall?

16) *Unit conversions*

a) $5\frac{1}{2}$ lb ≈ _____ kg

b) 87 cm ≈ _____ in

c) 3 pt ≈ _____ ml

d) 3.9 km ≈ _____ yd

e) 7 ft³ ≈ _____ m³

f) 26 m/s = _____ km/h

g) 1.8 g/cm³ ≈ _____ lb/ft³

17) A cylindrical pool has a 120 cm diameter and is 45 cm deep. What is the weight of the water in the pool?

18) A machine can pump 300 ℓ of water in 35 minutes. How much can it pump in 3 hours?

19) Patricia bikes up a 9 km hill averaging 6 km/h, and then bikes down the same hill at 45 km/h. What was her average speed for the whole trip?

End of Year Review – Sheet 2

1) Calculate the area.

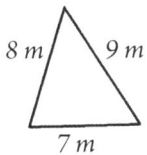

8 m, 9 m, 7 m

2) Calculate the length of the arc and the area of the segment.

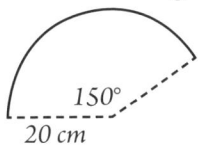

150°, 20 cm

3) Calculate the volume of this pyramid given that its height is 8 inches.

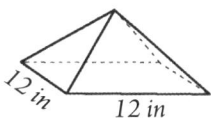

12 in, 12 in

4) Use the square root algorithm to calculate $\sqrt{42}$ (rounded to three significant digits).

5) What is 145% of 460?

6) What is 460 increased by 45%?

7) 950 is what percent of 7,600?

8) 98 is 56% of what?

9) 330 is 12% less than what?

10) What percentage decrease is it going from 1,500 down to 1,200?

11) The population of a town is about 10,000, and is increasing by 3.5% per year. What will its population be in 100 years, if that growth rate continues?

12) Kevin bought a house for £150,000 and then sold it for £200,000 five years later. What was the percentage profit?

13) Leslie bought a house for £200,000 and then sold it for £150,000 five years later. What was the percentage loss?

14) Ted is 60% taller than Fred.
 a) How tall is Fred if Ted is 140 cm tall?

 b) How tall is Ted if Fred is 140 cm tall?

15) Dan's investment account earns 8% APR. About how long does it take for his money to double?

16) What is the density (in g/cm^3) of a cube that weighs 5 kg and has edges that are 12 cm long?

17) What is the weight (in kg) of a solid cube of aluminum that has 20 cm long edges?

18) What is the volume (in cm^3) of 18 kg of iron?

19) A cylindrical tank has a height of 235 cm, a diameter of 110 cm. What is its volume:
 a) in cm^3?

 b) in m^3?

 c) in ft^3?

 d) in litres?

 e) in gallons?

 f) What is the weight of the water (in kg) when the tank is filled?

20) A map has a scale of 1 : 10 000. What is the real distance between two landmarks if they measure 4.2 cm apart on the map?

21) If it takes 6.8 gallons of petrol to drive 238 miles, how far can you drive on 16 gallons?

End of Year Review – Sheet 3

1) Calculate the area.

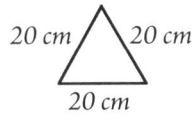

20 cm — 20 cm

20 cm

2) Calculate the volume.

26 cm

20 cm

3) A triangle has three sides measuring 23 cm, 51 cm and 57 cm. Is it an acute, an obtuse or a right triangle?

4) Use the square root algorithm to calculate $\sqrt{2639.9044}$. (It works out exactly!)

5) What is 94% of 4,200?

6) 250 is what percent of 400?

7) 400 is what percent of 250?

8) What percentage increase is it going from 280 to 330?

9) What percentage decrease is it going from 330 down to 280?

10) What is 17 decreased by 60%?

11) A house is purchased for £210,000. What will the value of the house be after 20 years, if it increases at a rate of 8.5% per year during that period?

12) Sophia's investment doubled over a 6-year period. Approximately, what was her average annual rate of return during this period?

13) Kevin has 20% more money than Dan. How much does Kevin have if Dan has £540?

14) Kevin has 20% more money than Dan. How much does Dan have if Kevin has £540?

15) Kevin has 20% less money than Dan. How much does Dan have if Kevin has £540?

16) A recipe calls for 50 mℓ of milk to make two dozen muffins. How much milk is needed in order to make 60 muffins?

17) It takes Sue 40 minutes to pick 7 baskets of apples. How long does it take her to pick 18 baskets?

18) *Unit conversions*

a) 7.3 oz ≈ _____ kg

b) 470 cm ≈ _____ yd

c) 0.39 ℓ ≈ _____ fl oz

d) 17 km² ≈ _____ mi²

e) 8 cm/s ≈ _____ mph

f) 63 kg/m³ = _____ g/cm³

19) A block of balsa wood has a volume of 0.42 m³. What does the block weigh given that balsa wood has a density of about 130 kg/m³?

20) A ball weighs 4.5 kg and is 20 cm in diameter. What is its density (in g/cm³)? Does it float or sink?

End of Year Review – Sheet 4

1) Find *x*, rounded to 3 significant digits. Use the square root algorithm.

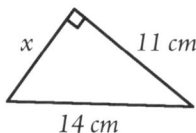

x   *11 cm*

14 cm

2) Calculate the area.

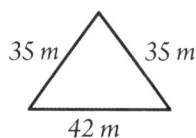

35 m   *35 m*

42 m

3) What is 350% of 40?

4) What is 800 increased by 0.4%?

5) 68 is what percent of 800?

6) 16.32 is 2.4% of what?

7) 6.3 is 28% less than what?

8) What percentage decrease is it going from 375 down to 90?

9) The population of a city is about 382,000 and is increasing by 3.4% per year. What will its population be in 30 years?

10) If the population of a country is growing at 4% per year, then about how long will it take the population to double?

11) Bob weighs 15% more than Pete. If Pete weighs 64 kg:
   a) How much does Bob weigh?

   b) What percent less does Pete weigh than Bob?

12) Pete weighs 15% less than Bob. If Pete weighs 64 kg:
   a) How much does Bob weigh?

   b) What percent more does Bob weigh than Pete?

13) After 50 minutes of shovelling, Jeff is $\frac{4}{5}$ of the way done with shoveling the snow from the sidewalk. How many more minutes will it be until he is finished?

14) On a map of the West Highland Way, the distance between Tyndrum and Bridge of Orchy measures 23.5 cm. The actual distance between these two places is 9.4 km.
   a) What is the verbal scale of the map?

   b) What is the fractional scale of the map?

   c) How many miles is one inch on the map?

15) A block measures 6 by 8 by 12 inches and weighs 30 lb. What is its density (in oz/in^3)?

16) A log has a density of 0.87 g/cm^3 and weighs 34.2 kg. What is its volume (in m^3)?

17) A standard football weighs 430 g and has a circumference of 70 cm. What would be the weight of a standard-sized football if it were solid gold?

18) A cube measures 35 cm along each edge, and is filled with water.
   a) What is the cube's capacity, in litres?

   b) What is the weight of the water?

19) A certain type of cheese sells for $4.80/lb in the U.S. and for €8.40/kg in Ireland. In which place is it cheaper, and what percentage of the Irish price is the U.S. price? (The exchange rates are $1.43/£ and €1.28/£.)

Multiplication Tables for Number Bases

Binary table

	0	1
0	0	0
1	0	1

Base-five table

	0	1	2	3	4
0	0	0	0	0	0
1	0	1	2	3	4
2	0	2	4	11	13
3	0	3	11	14	22
4	0	4	13	22	31

Base-eight table

	0	1	2	3	4	5	6	7
0	0	0	0	0	0	0	0	0
1	0	1	2	3	4	5	6	7
2	0	2	4	6	10	12	14	16
3	0	3	6	11	14	17	22	25
4	0	4	10	14	20	24	30	34
5	0	5	12	17	24	31	36	42
6	0	6	14	22	30	36	44	52
7	0	7	16	25	34	42	52	61

Hexadecimal times table

	0	1	2	3	4	5	6	7	8	9	A	B	C	D	E	F
0	0	0	0	0	0	0	0	0	0	0	0	0	0	0	0	0
1	0	1	2	3	4	5	6	7	8	9	A	B	C	D	E	F
2	0	2	4	6	8	A	C	E	10	12	14	16	18	1A	1C	1E
3	0	3	6	9	C	F	12	15	18	1B	1E	21	24	27	2A	2D
4	0	4	8	C	10	14	18	1C	20	24	28	2C	30	34	38	3C
5	0	5	A	F	14	19	1E	23	28	2D	32	37	3C	41	46	4B
6	0	6	C	12	18	1E	24	2A	30	36	3C	42	48	4E	54	5A
7	0	7	E	15	1C	23	2A	31	38	3F	46	4D	54	5B	62	69
8	0	8	10	18	20	28	30	38	40	48	50	58	60	68	70	78
9	0	9	12	1B	24	2D	36	3F	48	51	5A	63	6C	75	7E	87
A	0	A	14	1E	28	32	3C	46	50	5A	64	6E	78	82	8C	96
B	0	B	16	21	2C	37	42	4D	58	63	6E	79	84	8F	9A	A5
C	0	C	18	24	30	3C	48	54	60	6C	78	84	90	9C	A8	B4
D	0	D	1A	27	34	41	4E	5B	68	75	82	8F	9C	A9	B6	C3
E	0	E	1C	2A	38	46	54	62	70	7E	8C	9A	A8	B6	C4	D2
F	0	F	1E	2D	3C	4B	5A	69	78	87	96	A5	B4	C3	D2	E1

A Student's Workbook for Mathematics in Class 8

Place Value (exponent) Table

10	9	8	7	6	5	4	3	2	1	0	BASE
1024	512	256	128	64	32	16	8	4	2	1	2
					3125	625	125	25	5	1	5
					32768	4096	512	64	8	1	8
					100,000	10,000	1,000	100	10	1	10
						65536	4096	256	16	1	16

ASCII Code Table

Note: All codes are given in hexadecimal. Each hexadecimal digit can easily be converted to binary by using the table at the bottom of the page. For example, the character 'n' has an ASCII hexadecimal code 6E. Looking at the bottom of the page, we see that 6 is 0110 and that E is 1110. Therefore, the binary ASCII code for 'n' is 01101110. Note, also, that this table is incomplete. A full ASCII code table includes 256 codes, since there are 256 possible codes for one byte, which is an 8-digit binary code.

Hex	Char	Hex	Char	Hex	Char	Hex	Char	Hex	Char	Hex	Char
20	space	30	0	40	@	50	P	60	`	70	p
21	!	31	1	41	A	51	Q	61	a	71	q
22	'	32	2	42	B	52	R	62	b	72	r
23	#	33	3	43	C	53	S	63	c	73	s
24	$	34	4	44	D	54	T	64	d	74	t
25	%	35	5	45	E	55	U	65	e	75	u
26	&	36	6	46	F	56	V	66	f	76	v
27	'	37	7	47	G	57	W	67	g	77	w
28	(	38	8	48	H	58	x	68	h	78	x
29	)	39	9	49	I	59	y	69	i	79	y
2A	*	3A	:	4A	J	5A	z	6A	j	7A	z
2B	+	3B	;	4B	K	5B	[	6B	k	7B	{
2C	,	3C	<	4C	L	5C	\	6C	l	7C	|
2D	–	3D	=	4D	M	5D	]	6D	m	7D	}
2E	.	3E	>	4E	N	5E	^	6E	n	7E	~
2F	/	3F	?	4F	O	5F	_	6F	o	7F	del

Binary/Hexadecimal Conversion Table

Binary	Hexadecimal	Binary	Hexadecimal
0000	0	1000	8
0001	1	1001	9
0010	2	1010	A
0011	3	1011	B
0100	4	1100	C
0101	5	1101	D
0110	6	1110	E
0111	7	1111	F

Table of Squares

$1^2 = 1$	$27^2 = 729$	$53^2 = 2809$	$79^2 = 6241$
$2^2 = 4$	$28^2 = 784$	$54^2 = 2916$	$80^2 = 6400$
$3^2 = 9$	$29^2 = 841$	$55^2 = 3025$	$81^2 = 6561$
$4^2 = 16$	$30^2 = 900$	$56^2 = 3136$	$82^2 = 6724$
$5^2 = 25$	$31^2 = 961$	$57^2 = 3249$	$83^2 = 6889$
$6^2 = 36$	$32^2 = 1024$	$58^2 = 3364$	$84^2 = 7056$
$7^2 = 49$	$33^2 = 1089$	$59^2 = 3481$	$85^2 = 7225$
$8^2 = 64$	$34^2 = 1156$	$60^2 = 3600$	$86^2 = 7396$
$9^2 = 81$	$35^2 = 1225$	$61^2 = 3721$	$87^2 = 7569$
$10^2 = 100$	$36^2 = 1296$	$62^2 = 3844$	$88^2 = 7744$
$11^2 = 121$	$37^2 = 1369$	$63^2 = 3969$	$89^2 = 7921$
$12^2 = 144$	$38^2 = 1444$	$64^2 = 4096$	$90^2 = 8100$
$13^2 = 169$	$39^2 = 1521$	$65^2 = 4225$	$91^2 = 8281$
$14^2 = 196$	$40^2 = 1600$	$66^2 = 4356$	$92^2 = 8464$
$15^2 = 225$	$41^2 = 1681$	$67^2 = 4489$	$93^2 = 8649$
$16^2 = 256$	$42^2 = 1764$	$68^2 = 4624$	$94^2 = 8836$
$17^2 = 289$	$43^2 = 1849$	$69^2 = 4761$	$95^2 = 9025$
$18^2 = 324$	$44^2 = 1936$	$70^2 = 4900$	$96^2 = 9216$
$19^2 = 361$	$45^2 = 2025$	$71^2 = 5041$	$97^2 = 9409$
$20^2 = 400$	$46^2 = 2116$	$72^2 = 5184$	$98^2 = 9604$
$21^2 = 441$	$47^2 = 2209$	$73^2 = 5329$	$99^2 = 9801$
$22^2 = 484$	$48^2 = 2304$	$74^2 = 5476$	$100^2 = 10,000$
$23^2 = 529$	$49^2 = 2401$	$75^2 = 5625$	
$24^2 = 576$	$50^2 = 2500$	$76^2 = 5776$	
$25^2 = 625$	$51^2 = 2601$	$77^2 = 5929$	
$26^2 = 676$	$52^2 = 2704$	$78^2 = 6084$	

A Student's Workbook for Mathematics in Class 8

Table of Square Roots

$\sqrt{1} = 1.000$	$\sqrt{27} = 5.196$	$\sqrt{53} = 7.280$	$\sqrt{79} = 8.888$
$\sqrt{2} = 1.414$	$\sqrt{28} = 5.292$	$\sqrt{54} = 7.348$	$\sqrt{80} = 8.944$
$\sqrt{3} = 1.732$	$\sqrt{29} = 5.385$	$\sqrt{55} = 7.416$	$\sqrt{81} = 9.000$
$\sqrt{4} = 2.000$	$\sqrt{30} = 5.477$	$\sqrt{56} = 7.483$	$\sqrt{82} = 9.055$
$\sqrt{5} = 2.236$	$\sqrt{31} = 5.568$	$\sqrt{57} = 7.550$	$\sqrt{83} = 9.110$
$\sqrt{6} = 2.449$	$\sqrt{32} = 5.657$	$\sqrt{58} = 7.616$	$\sqrt{84} = 9.165$
$\sqrt{7} = 2.646$	$\sqrt{33} = 5.745$	$\sqrt{59} = 7.681$	$\sqrt{85} = 9.220$
$\sqrt{8} = 2.828$	$\sqrt{34} = 5.831$	$\sqrt{60} = 7.746$	$\sqrt{86} = 9.274$
$\sqrt{9} = 3.000$	$\sqrt{35} = 5.916$	$\sqrt{61} = 7.810$	$\sqrt{87} = 9.327$
$\sqrt{10} = 3.162$	$\sqrt{36} = 6.000$	$\sqrt{62} = 7.874$	$\sqrt{88} = 9.381$
$\sqrt{11} = 3.317$	$\sqrt{37} = 6.083$	$\sqrt{63} = 7.937$	$\sqrt{89} = 9.434$
$\sqrt{12} = 3.464$	$\sqrt{38} = 6.164$	$\sqrt{64} = 8.000$	$\sqrt{90} = 9.487$
$\sqrt{13} = 3.606$	$\sqrt{39} = 6.245$	$\sqrt{65} = 8.062$	$\sqrt{91} = 9.539$
$\sqrt{14} = 3.742$	$\sqrt{40} = 6.325$	$\sqrt{66} = 8.124$	$\sqrt{92} = 9.592$
$\sqrt{15} = 3.873$	$\sqrt{41} = 6.403$	$\sqrt{67} = 8.185$	$\sqrt{93} = 9.644$
$\sqrt{16} = 4.000$	$\sqrt{42} = 6.481$	$\sqrt{68} = 8.246$	$\sqrt{94} = 9.695$
$\sqrt{17} = 4.123$	$\sqrt{43} = 6.557$	$\sqrt{69} = 8.307$	$\sqrt{95} = 9.747$
$\sqrt{18} = 4.243$	$\sqrt{44} = 6.633$	$\sqrt{70} = 8.367$	$\sqrt{96} = 9.798$
$\sqrt{19} = 4.359$	$\sqrt{45} = 6.708$	$\sqrt{71} = 8.426$	$\sqrt{97} = 9.849$
$\sqrt{20} = 4.472$	$\sqrt{46} = 6.782$	$\sqrt{72} = 8.485$	$\sqrt{98} = 9.899$
$\sqrt{21} = 4.583$	$\sqrt{47} = 6.856$	$\sqrt{73} = 8.544$	$\sqrt{99} = 9.950$
$\sqrt{22} = 4.690$	$\sqrt{48} = 6.928$	$\sqrt{74} = 8.602$	$\sqrt{100} = 10.000$
$\sqrt{23} = 4.796$	$\sqrt{49} = 7.000$	$\sqrt{75} = 8.660$	
$\sqrt{24} = 4.899$	$\sqrt{50} = 7.071$	$\sqrt{76} = 8.718$	
$\sqrt{25} = 5.000$	$\sqrt{51} = 7.141$	$\sqrt{77} = 8.775$	
$\sqrt{26} = 5.099$	$\sqrt{52} = 7.211$	$\sqrt{78} = 8.832$	

Note: If there are ending zeroes inside the square root, then you can remove an even number of zeroes from inside, which will result in half as many zeroes (or moving the decimal place half as many places) in your answer.

Examples:

With $\sqrt{25,000,000}$ we remove 6 zeroes, then adding 3 zeroes to $\sqrt{25}$, gives an answer of 5,000.

With $\sqrt{60,000}$ we remove 4 zeroes. Since $\sqrt{6}$ is 2.449, we move 2 decimal places to get 244.9.

With $\sqrt{600,000}$ we remove 4 zeroes. Since $\sqrt{60}$ is 7.746, we move 2 decimal places to get 774.6.

Note: This table should not be used if, after removing an *even* number of zeroes, there are more than two digits inside the square root. For example, it *can* be used for $\sqrt{58,000,000}$, but *cannot* be used for $\sqrt{58,700}$ or for $\sqrt{580}$ or for $\sqrt{5,800,000}$.

Growth Rate Table

giving values for $(1 + r)^t$ from the formula $P = P_0(1 + r)^t$

t	1.01	1.02	1.025	1.03	1.035	1.04	1.05	1.06	1.07	1.08	1.09	1.1	1.15	1.2	1.25	1.3	1.4	1.5	2
2	1.0201	1.0404	1.05063	1.0609	1.07123	1.0816	1.1025	1.1236	1.1449	1.1664	1.1881	1.21	1.3225	1.44	1.5625	1.69	1.96	2.25	4
3	1.0303	1.06121	1.07689	1.09273	1.10872	1.12486	1.15763	1.19102	1.22504	1.25971	1.29503	1.331	1.52088	1.728	1.95313	2.197	2.744	3.375	8
4	1.0406	1.08243	1.10381	1.12551	1.14752	1.16986	1.21551	1.26248	1.3108	1.36049	1.41158	1.4641	1.74901	2.0736	2.44141	2.8561	3.8416	5.0625	16
5	1.05101	1.10408	1.13141	1.15927	1.18769	1.21665	1.27628	1.33823	1.40255	1.46933	1.53862	1.61051	2.01136	2.48832	3.05176	3.71293	5.37824	7.59375	32
6	1.06152	1.12616	1.15969	1.19405	1.22926	1.26532	1.3401	1.41852	1.50073	1.58687	1.6771	1.77156	2.31306	2.98598	3.8147	4.82681	7.52954	11.3906	64
7	1.07214	1.14869	1.18869	1.22987	1.27228	1.31593	1.4071	1.50363	1.60578	1.71382	1.82804	1.94872	2.66002	3.58318	4.76837	6.27485	10.5414	17.0859	128
8	1.08286	1.17166	1.2184	1.26677	1.31681	1.36857	1.47746	1.59385	1.71819	1.85093	1.99256	2.14359	3.05902	4.29982	5.96046	8.15731	14.7579	25.6289	256
9	1.09369	1.19509	1.24886	1.30477	1.3629	1.42331	1.55133	1.68948	1.83846	1.999	2.17189	2.35795	3.51788	5.15978	7.45058	10.6045	20.661	38.4434	512
10	1.10462	1.21899	1.28008	1.34392	1.4106	1.48024	1.62889	1.79085	1.96715	2.15892	2.36736	2.59374	4.04556	6.19174	9.31323	13.7858	28.9255	57.665	1024
11	1.11567	1.24337	1.31209	1.38423	1.45997	1.53945	1.71034	1.8983	2.10485	2.33164	2.58043	2.85312	4.65239	7.43008	11.6415	17.9216	40.4957	86.4976	2048
12	1.12683	1.26824	1.34489	1.42576	1.51107	1.60103	1.79586	2.0122	2.25219	2.51817	2.81266	3.13843	5.35025	8.9161	14.5519	23.2981	56.6939	129.746	4096
13	1.13809	1.29361	1.37851	1.46853	1.56396	1.66507	1.88565	2.13293	2.40985	2.71962	3.0658	3.45227	6.15279	10.6993	18.1899	30.2875	79.3715	194.62	8192
14	1.14947	1.31948	1.41297	1.51259	1.61869	1.73168	1.97993	2.2609	2.57853	2.93719	3.34173	3.7975	7.07571	12.8392	22.7374	39.3738	111.12	291.929	16384
15	1.16097	1.34587	1.4483	1.55797	1.67535	1.80094	2.07893	2.39656	2.75903	3.17217	3.64248	4.17725	8.13706	15.407	28.4217	51.1859	155.568	437.894	32768
16	1.17258	1.37279	1.48451	1.60471	1.73399	1.87298	2.18287	2.54035	2.95216	3.42594	3.97031	4.59497	9.35762	18.4884	35.5271	66.5417	217.795	656.841	65536
17	1.1843	1.40024	1.52162	1.65285	1.79468	1.9479	2.29202	2.69277	3.15882	3.70002	4.32763	5.05447	10.7613	22.1861	44.4089	86.5042	304.913	985.261	131072
18	1.19615	1.42825	1.55966	1.70243	1.85749	2.02582	2.40662	2.85434	3.37993	3.99602	4.71712	5.55992	12.3755	26.6233	55.5112	112.455	426.879	1477.89	262144
19	1.20811	1.45681	1.59865	1.75351	1.9225	2.10685	2.52695	3.0256	3.61653	4.3157	5.14166	6.11591	14.2318	31.948	69.3889	146.192	597.63	2216.84	524288
20	1.22019	1.48595	1.63862	1.80611	1.98979	2.19112	2.6533	3.20714	3.86968	4.66096	5.60441	6.7275	16.3665	38.3376	86.7362	190.05	836.683	3325.26	1048576
25	1.28243	1.64061	1.85394	2.09378	2.36324	2.66584	3.38635	4.29187	5.42743	6.84848	8.62308	10.8347	32.919	95.3962	264.698	705.641	4499.88	25251.2	3.4E+07
30	1.34785	1.81136	2.09757	2.42726	2.80679	3.2434	4.32194	5.74349	7.61226	10.0627	13.2677	17.4494	66.2118	237.376	807.794	2620	24201.4	191751	1.1E+09
40	1.48886	2.20804	2.68506	3.26204	3.95926	4.80102	7.03999	10.2857	14.9745	21.7245	31.4094	45.2593	267.864	1469.77	7523.16	36118.9	700038	1.1E+07	1.1E+12
50	1.64463	2.69159	3.43711	4.38391	5.58493	7.10668	11.4674	18.4202	29.457	46.9016	74.3575	117.391	1083.66	9100.44	70064.9	497929	2E+07	6.4E+08	1.1E+15
60	1.8167	3.28103	4.39979	5.8916	7.87809	10.5196	18.6792	32.9877	57.9464	101.257	176.031	304.482	4384	56347.5	652530	6864377	5.9E+08	3.7E+10	1.2E+18
80	2.21672	4.87544	7.20957	10.6409	15.6757	23.0498	49.5614	105.796	224.234	471.955	986.552	2048.4	71750.9	2160228	5.7E+07	1.3E+09	4.9E+11	1.2E+14	1.2E+24
100	2.70481	7.24465	11.8137	19.2186	31.1914	50.5049	131.501	339.302	867.716	2199.76	5529.04	13780.6	1174313	8.3E+07	4.9E+09	2.5E+11	4.1E+14	1.3E+17	1.3E+30
150	4.44842	19.4996	40.605	84.2527	174.202	358.923	1507.98	6250	25560.3	103172	411126	1617718	1.3E+09	7.5E+11	3.4E+14	1.2E+17	8.3E+21	2.6E+26	1.4E+45
200	7.31602	52.4849	139.564	369.356	972.904	2550.75	17292.6	115126	752932	4838950	3.1E+07	1.9E+08	1.4E+12	6.9E+15	2.4E+19	6.1E+22	1.7E+29	1.6E+35	1.6E+60

$(1 + r)$

Note: The cell on the bottom right $(1.6E + 60)$ means 1.6×10^{60} in scientific notation. The last column is where $(r + 1)$ is 2, or $r = 1$, which means 100% annual growth, or doubling.

A Student's Workbook for Mathematics in Class 8

Conversion Table
Measure and conversion tables
Metric system
Weight
1 tonne = 1,000 kilograms (kg)
1 kg = 1,000 grams (g)
1 g = 1,000 milligrams (mg)

Length
1 kilometre (km) = 1,000 metres (m)
1 m = 100 centimetres (cm)
1 m = 1,000 millimetres (mm)

Area
1 km^2 = 100 hectares (ha)
1 ha = $10,000 \text{ m}^2$ (100×100 m)
1 m^2 = $10,000 \text{ cm}^2$
1 cm^2 = 100 mm^2

Volume
1 m^3 = $1,000,000 \text{ cm}^3$
1 m^3 = 1,000 litres (ℓ)
1ℓ = $1,000 \text{ cm}^3$ ($10 \times 10 \times 10$ cm)
1ℓ = $1,000 \text{ m}\ell \text{ cm}^3$ ($10 \times 10 \times 10$ cm)
$1 \text{ m}\ell$ = 1 cm^3

Speed
1 km/h $\approx$ 0.278 m/s
1 m/s = 3.6 km/h

Density
1 g/cm^3 = $1 \text{ kg}/\ell$ = $1,000 \text{ kg/m}^3$

Imperial system
Weight
1 stone (st) = 14 pounds (lb)
1 lb = 16 ounces (oz)

Length
1 mile (mi) = 1,760 yards (yd)
1 mi = 5,280 feet (ft)
1 yd = 3 ft
1 ft = 12 inches (in)

Area
1 mi^2 = 640 acres
1 acre = $4,840 \text{ yd}^2$
1 yd^2 = 9 ft^2
1 ft^2 = 144 in^2

Volume
1 gallon (gal) = 8 pints (pt)
1 pt = 20 fluid ounces (fl oz)*
1 ft^3 = $1,728 \text{ in}^3$

Speed
1 mph $\approx$ 1.467 ft/s
1 ft/s $\approx$ 0.682 mph

Density
1 oz/in^3 = 108 lb/ft^3

Conversion to metric
Weight
1 st $\approx$ 6.35 kg
1 lb $\approx$ 454 g
1 oz $\approx$ 28.35 g

Length
1 mi $\approx$ 1.6093 km
1 yd $\approx$ 91.44 cm
1 ft $\approx$ 30.48 cm
1 in $\approx$ 2.54 cm

Area
$1 \text{ mi}^2 \approx 2.59 \text{ km}^2$
1 acre $\approx$ 0.405 ha
$1 \text{ yd}^2 \approx 0.836 \text{ m}^2$
$1 \text{ ft}^2 \approx 0.0929 \text{ m} \approx 929 \text{ cm}^2$
$1 \text{ in}^2 \approx 6.452 \text{ cm}^2$

---

* The US pint is only 16 fl oz, so a US pint and gallon is smaller than imperial. The US gallon is about 3.785 ℓ. (The imperial and US fl oz is also not exactly the same.)

Volume
1 (imp) gal ≈ 4.546 ℓ
1 pt ≈ 568.25 mℓ
1 fl oz ≈ 28.41 mℓ
1 ft³ ≈ 0.0283 m³
1 in³ ≈ 16.387 cm³

Speed
1 mph ≈ 1.6093 km/h ≈ 0.4470 m/s
1 ft/s ≈ 0.3048 m/s ≈ 1.097 km/h

Density
1 oz/in³ ≈ 1.73 g/cm³
1 lb/ft³ ≈ 16.02 kg/m³

Temperature
$C = \frac{5}{9}(F - 32)$

Conversion to imperial
Weight
1 kg ≈ 2.2046 (2.2) lb
1 g ≈ .0353 oz

Length
1 km ≈ 0.6214 mi
1 m ≈ 1.094 yd
1 m ≈ 3.281 ft
1 cm ≈ 0.39370 in

Area
1 km² ≈ 0.386 mi²
1 ha ≈ 2.471 acre
1 m² ≈ 1.196 yd²
1 m² ≈ 10.764 ft²
1 cm² ≈ 0.155 in²

Volume
1 ℓ ≈ 0.220 (imp) gal
1 ℓ ≈ 1.76 pt
1 ℓ ≈ 35.2 fl oz
1 m³ ≈ 35.314 ft³
1 cm³ ≈ 0.0610 in³

Speed
1 km/h ≈ 0.6214 mph ≈ 0.9114 ft/s
1 m/s ≈ 3.281 ft/s ≈ 2.237 mph

Density
1 g/cm³ ≈ 0.578 oz/in³
1 kg/m³ ≈ 62.43 lb/ft³

Temperature
$F = \frac{9}{5}(C + 32)$

Density of some materials
Water (at a maximum density of 4°C)
   1 g/cm³ = 1 kg/ℓ = 1,000 kg/m³ (0.578
   oz/in³, 62.43 lb/ft³)
Air 1.29 kg/m³ 1.29 oz/ft³ –
   coincidentally!)
Aluminium 2.70 g/cm³ (169 lb/ft³)
Iron 7.10 g/cm³ (443 lb/ft³)
Mercury 13.5 g/cm³ (843 lb/ft³)
Gold 19.3 g/cm³ (1,204 lb/ft³)

Formulas
Volume of a cylinder or prism: $V = A_{\text{base}} \times h$
Volume of a pyramid or cone: $V = \frac{1}{3}A_{\text{base}} \times h$
Volume of a sphere: $V = \frac{4}{3}\pi r^3$
Surface area of a sphere: $S = 4\pi r^2$

Heron's formula
The area of a triangle is:

$$A = \sqrt{s(s-a)(s-b)(s-c)}$$

where a, b, c are the sides of the triangle, and
   s is the semi-perimeter (i.e., half the
   length of the perimeter).

MAKING MATHS MEANINGFUL

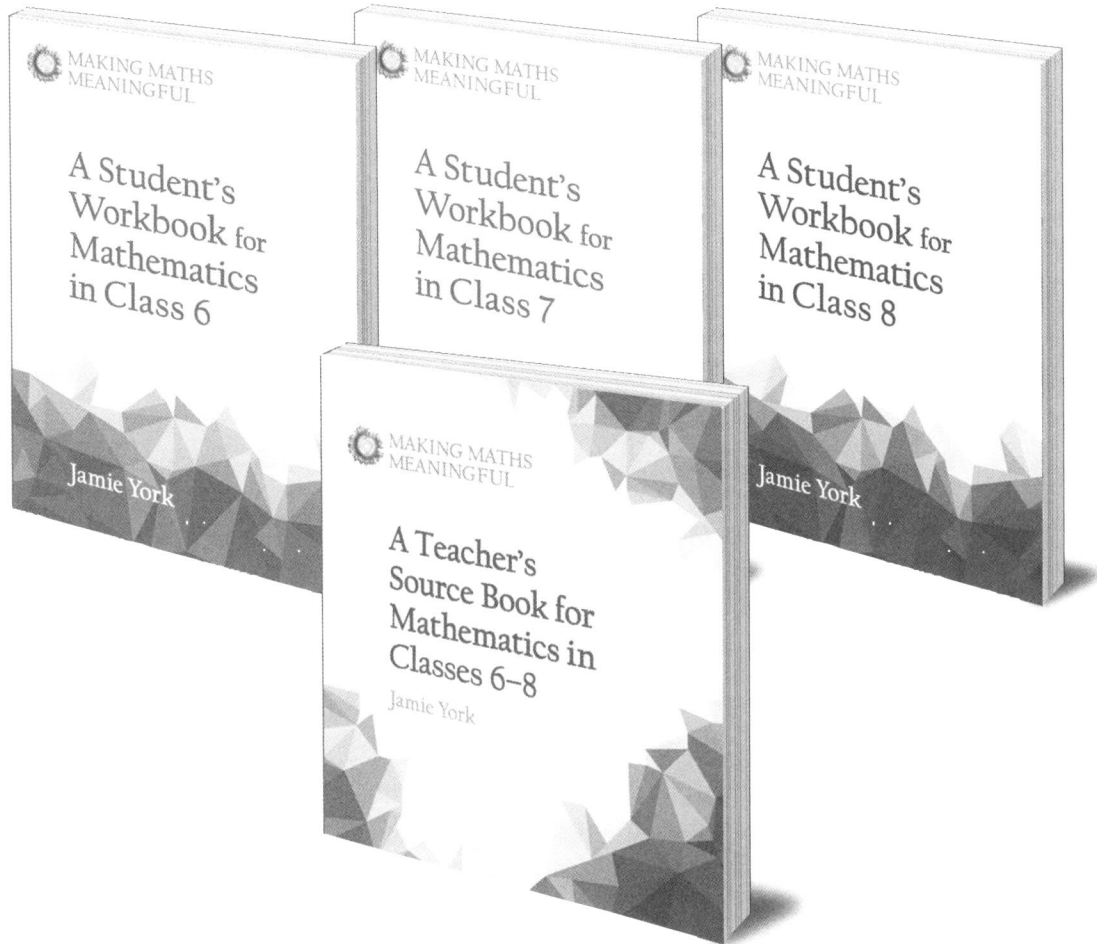

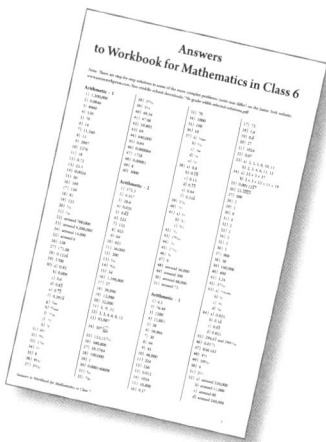

A Student's Workbook for Mathematics in Class 6
Jamie York

A Student's Workbook for Mathematics in Class 7
Jamie York

A Student's Workbook for Mathematics in Class 8
Jamie York

A Teacher's Source Book for Mathematics in Classes 6–8
Jamie York

Jamie York's unique maths workbooks are available for Classes 6, 7 and 8, alongside a comprehensive teacher's book for all three years.

Workbooks are also available in classroom packs of 10 copies with a teacher's answer booklet.

"Jamie York has helped me develop students who are on the path to becoming imaginative, analytical thinkers in high school."
– Waldorf teacher, Portland, Oregon

florisbooks.co.uk

First published in the United States of America
by Jamie York Press, Boulder CO in 2009
www.JamieYorkPress.com
First published in the UK in 2016
by Floris Books, Edinburgh,
adapted from the 2015 American edition

British Library CIP Data available
ISBN 978-178250-321-7
Printed in Great Britain
by Bell & Bain Ltd